the sh*t
taught y

attitude.

Vision | Change | Learning | Fear | Boldness

Adam Ashton & Adam Jones

Attitude
Copyright © 2023 by Adam Jones and Adam Ashton.
All rights reserved. No part of this book may be used or reproduced or transmitted in any form or by any means, electronic, or mechanical, including photocopying, recording, or by any information storage or retrieval system, without permission from the copyright owner.
Rev. date: 01/05/2023

For information contact:
book@theshittheynevertaughtyou.com
www.whatyouwilllearn.com

Edited by Skye Hughes
Cover Design by Jack Turner
Audiobook Production by Jan Wong
Print Layout by Tash Simmons
eBook Layout by Gareth Clegg

ISBN: 978-0-6451338-3-7
First Edition: May 2023

contents.

Introduction	**4**
Lesson 1: Vision	**10**
Chapter 1: Following The Heart	*12*
Chapter 2: Peak Experience	*22*
Chapter 3: Keys to Fulfilment	*30*
Lesson 2: Change	**40**
Chapter 4: The Beach Bum and The Millionaire	*42*
Chapter 5: Overcoming Obstacles To Change	*52*
Chapter 6: Making Diamonds	*64*
Lesson 3: Learning	**74**
Chapter 7: Meta-Learning	*76*
Chapter 8: Get Off The Couch	*86*
Chapter 9: Deep Practice	*94*

Lesson 4: Fear   **110**

Chapter 10: Fear Reframe #1: *WHY Do You Fear?*   *112*

Chapter 11: Fear Reframe #2: *WHAT Do You Fear?*   *124*

Chapter 12: The Most Significant Struggle   *132*

Lesson 5: Boldness   **138**

Chapter 13: Bold Mofo #1: Richard Branson   *140*

Chapter 14: Bold Mofo #2: David Goggins   *148*

Chapter 15: Bold Mofo #3: Malala Yousafzai   *158*

Chapter 16: Components of Boldness   *172*

Conclusion   **180**

Chapter 17: Take Your Turn   *182*

introduction.

INTRODUCTION

Have you ever heard something so simple yet so profound that it made you say: *"Why the hell didn't someone teach me that earlier?!"* We have. And it didn't just happen once - it happens every few weeks.

We're avid readers. Adam Ashton, a marketer currently preparing for his first child, and Adam Jones, an engineer currently building his first software company. Back in 2016, we started a podcast called *What You Will Learn*, where we read a book each week and share the best bits and the biggest lessons.

After reading awe-inspiring stories about some of history's greatest individuals, we wanted to work out what set them apart. We dug deep into the lives of entrepreneurs, CEOs, thought-leaders, politicians, musicians and artists to uncover what made them so successful. Did they begin the race with a head start, born with advantages that made their success inevitable?

The more we tried to identify a common leg-up, the more it seemed that each faced their own unique challenges in life. Often they faced oppression, abuse, poverty, or a myriad of other obstacles... it seems they didn't succeed *thanks* to their upbringing, but rather *in spite* of it.

The only thing they all had in common? Their *attitude*. And fortunately for us, our attitude is something we can control.

Whatever you hope to achieve in life, the right attitude is crucial to getting you there.

INTRODUCTION

What Lies Ahead

This book is a deep dive into all things *Attitude*. We've identified the best books on this topic and extracted the best ideas to come up with five vital lessons - with one meta-conclusion.

Here's what you can expect:

- *Vision:* The first step in *getting* to where you want to go is *knowing* where you want to go in the first place. Over the next few years, you're going to get somewhere... but unless you set a bit of a vision for yourself, the place you end up may not be the place you wanted to go.
- *Change:* Having crafted your vision, you might realise that there's a little bit of a gap between where you are now and where you want to be. Or perhaps more than a *little bit* of a gap... In order to close that gap, to move closer towards the person you want to be, you're going to need to change. Change can be scary. It means moving into unknown territories. It means moving outside your comfort zone, outside of the warm and safe place you know. But if you want to improve, change will be an inevitable part of the journey.
- *Learning:* As you're working toward your vision and making changes in your life, you will have to try new things. Things you've never done before, things you never thought you could do, but things that are

INTRODUCTION

vital to achieving your goals. There are times when we must learn new things (a new course, a new job, new software, a new hobby), but most of us don't have an intentional approach to learning. Thankfully, Lesson 3 offers new frameworks for learning and new mindsets you can apply to the struggle it takes to get from *being* shit to *holy* shit[1].

- *Fear:* So far, everything might sound pretty exciting. But it might also sound a little scary. Thinking about your future is scary, change is scary, learning new things is scary. Lesson 4 provides new ways to reframe fear into something that will help propel you forward rather than hold you back.
- *Boldness:* The last piece of the *Attitude* puzzle is that little bit of grunt, that little bit of scrappiness, that brash confidence to just get out there and have a crack. In spite of fears, in spite of not knowing exactly what to do or how to do it, a little bit of boldness might be the last thing you need to get you off the sidelines and into the arena.

---

[1] Pretty happy with that gag, it will make sense when you read Chapter 9.

INTRODUCTION

A quick side note about our previous book:
After reading over 300 books and experiencing hundreds of forehead-slapping moments from learning something new and amazing, we decided to compile a whole bunch of those lessons into a book of our own. Launched in May 2021, reaching a whopping 684 pages, *The Sh*t They Never Taught You* was a combination of the best ideas from 115 different books, grouped into 32 meta-lessons across 9 different categories. It took us about 16 months to write[2]. It was the best thing we'd ever done - taking hundreds of books, picking out the best bits, grouping them together with similar ideas, and making it relatable and easy to understand.

But since then, we've read more. And we've experienced more and more of those *"why did no one ever tell us this"* moments. So we decided to put all these new lessons together in this book! And this time, we're going to the opposite end of the spectrum. Instead of almost 700 pages, we aimed to keep it under 200. Instead of over 100 different books, we wanted this one to have less than 20. Instead of

---

[2] Well, it took us about a month and a half to *write*... then when Jonesy infamously said: *"I think we're about 95% done,"* it took another 15 months to re-write it all, then edit it down, then chuck the whole thing in the bin and completely start over from scratch.

going wide across a bunch of different lessons, we wanted to go deep on a small handful of interrelated ones. Instead of being broad and general, we wanted this one to be narrow and specific.

If you enjoy reading this book and learn some valuable lessons, we might end up with a whole suite of narrow, specific books to complement the yellow monster. The big boy allows you to get an overview of the whole landscape; then, these smaller companions let you zoom in on specific areas relevant to you.

The most important thing to us was that we wanted this new book to be ultra-useful to a specific important area of life, and we didn't want this to feel like a 'cash grab' in any way. We've seen it before - an author takes two or three of their old books and combines bits and pieces into a 'new' one... that doesn't really feel new at all. That's not for us.

This book is composed of *entirely new content*. In selecting the lessons and ideas that went into the book you're holding, we started with the assumption that everything we wrote about in *The Sh*t They Never Taught You* was out of consideration.

Attitude and *The Sh*t They Never Taught You* aren't mutually exclusive; they complement each other. The whole is greater than the sum of its parts.

Lesson 1

vision.

LESSON 1 | *Vision*

A project team who had successfully completed the most beautiful building in the city got together to celebrate their creation. After a few pints, the discussion got heated about who had the most important role.

The engineer went first: *"Well, clearly it is I. Without my intelligence, the building would not be able to withstand the loads of gravity."*

Next was the project manager who claimed: *"But if it weren't for me, you lot would still be tweaking designs - nothing would have been done on time or on budget."*

Finally, the architect landed the death blow: *"Without my vision of the exquisite form, this building may have been well managed and well-engineered. But it would be totally bland and boring. It would've been indistinguishable from all the other buildings around us."*

When designing our own lives, we don't have the luxury of having a whole team to conjure up something great. We need to be able to deploy all roles for ourselves.

Too often, we focus on being successful "doers," pragmatically executing tasks to the best of our ability. But if we don't take the time to step back and envision exactly what we want, unique to who we are, we're destined to be just another bland and indistinguishable human in the sea of sameness.

LESSON 1 | *Vision*

CHAPTER 1
Following The Heart

"The secret of life, though, is to fall seven times and to get up eight."

Inspired by: **The Alchemist,** *by Paulo Coelho*

Santiago is a young boy from Spain. He begins his (fictional) journey as a simple sheepherder, yet also an ambitious explorer. He is content with his life; however, he also experiences vivid dreams about the Egyptian pyramids. Most of us would pass these dreams off as random and meaningless, but Santiago felt they were trying to tell him something. He thought they were calling to him, trying to show him a path. He believed they were his 'Personal Legend.' In other words, he had this sense that going to the pyramids was the reason for his existence.

But how could he be so certain? He was comfortable at home, and so he faced the choice: stay with the safe and certain life of a shepherd... or follow his heart and chase his dream?

LESSON 1 | *Vision*

Santiago, the young whippersnapper, decided to go for it[3]. He wanted to see the fields, the countryside and the places where the grass was greener. As soon as he left his local neighbourhood, he experienced a sense of freedom like never before; he was happy.

Although he no longer had security, he was able to live his dream. Santiago learnt early on his journey that: *"It's the possibility of having a dream come true that makes life interesting."*

He met others on a similar path and was assured that: *"When you really want something, the universe conspires in helping you achieve it."*

Santi crossed the Strait of Gibraltar en route to Morocco and soon found himself lost in an unfamiliar marketplace with unfamiliar people speaking an unfamiliar language. Luckily, he found a nice bloke who offered to help him cross the Sahara to reach Egypt - all they needed to do first was buy a camel. Santiago handed his cash over to this lad, convinced he could negotiate the best deal as he spoke the language and knew the bazaar well. The two of them journeyed through the marketplace, searching for a bargain on a pair of camels. To Santiago's dismay, the other lad wove his way into a crowd and never popped out the other side... he'd bolted with the cash!

Now Santi found himself in an even worse predicament - an unknown land, an unknown language, and pockets

---

[3] You probably could have predicted that one - big Paulo would've struggled to get a book out of it if Santi just hung out with his sheep.

that were now empty. He was only on the very first leg of his journey, and the world had already smacked him with serious obstacles.

He had another choice to make. The same choice as before but with new stakes: does he *go back* to his old life of comfort and security, or, despite losing everything but the shirt on his back, keep moving forward in the pursuit of his dream?

About Alchemy

Courageously, he decided to continue in his pursuit of his Personal Legend[4], despite some inclination that this whole dream could be a sham.

As Santi's journey continued, things did not get easier. He was constantly subjected to tests of his persistence and courage. Despite this, he remained steadfast in his pursuit and continued to work tirelessly from dawn to dusk. Santi figured that these challenges were inevitable for all explorers when they take the plunge and dare to venture out on their own. While at times it felt like pushing shit uphill, it was through these challenges he learned his most valuable lesson: *Alchemy*.

Alchemy is a pretty cool profession. The story goes that if you have a philosopher's stone, you can turn any base metal (such as lead or copper) into gold. Anyone that could do this would be a pretty well-off individual. Imagine just picking

---

[4] Again, probably $1.01 odds on that one - would've been a pretty weak book if he just turned around and went home at the first hurdle.

LESSON 1 | *Vision*

up your knife and fork for your evening meal, clicking your fingers and turning them to gold.

It sounds made up, but *true* alchemy does exist. Sadly, most people will never get to experience how it really works. Alchemy in our world is not about literally making gold - it's about discovering our Personal Legend, about uncovering the treasure that has been reserved for each and every one of us.

The mistake most people make is hoping to uncover it instantly, like the click of a finger that turns your cutlery to gold. They don't realise there are steps along the way to their metaphorical gold. There are evolutions you need to make on your journey.

Most wannabe 'alchemists' are seeking their treasure, the pot of gold at the end of the rainbow, without wanting to actually walk along the rainbow. They want the reward for *reaching* the reason for their existence without actually *pursuing* it. Becoming wholeheartedly aligned to your Personal Legend is a process of gradual transformation, and only true alchemists understand what it means to make the necessary evolutions along the way to secure their treasure.

In pursuing his dream, Santiago had already made a few of his evolutions. He was on his way to living out the transformative life of a true Alchemist.

LESSON 1 | *Vision*

The Final Evolution

On his journey, Santiago was transitioning from a pretty lame base metal to something a bit more upmarket in the periodic table. The further he progressed on his journey, the better things seemed to turn out. Plenty of perks began to appear: he got rich with (literal) gold, got a hot desert girlfriend, was living his purpose, and even met another Alchemist. Despite nailing it by most desirable metrics, he knew deep down he still hadn't reached the full extent of his Personal Legend: the pyramids.

So, again, he faced another choice. This required equal courage, but for different reasons. Previously, he had nothing to lose and everything to gain. This time, he had everything to lose. He had transformed far beyond the simple shepherd boy he was before he began his journey. Luckily, he sought wise counsel from his more experienced fellow Alchemist pal, who described what happens when you stop chasing your dream before you reach it:

> *"Let me tell you what will happen:*
> *You'll be the counsellor of the Oasis.*
> *You will have enough money to buy many sheep and camels.*
> *You'll marry Fatimah, and you'll be happy for a year.*
> *You'll learn to love the desert, and you'll get to know every one of the fifty thousand palm trees.*

LESSON 1 | *Vision*

You'll watch them as they grow, and you'll get better at understanding omens of the desert."

Things are sounding pretty good so far.
But then he continued:

"Sometime during the second year you'll remember the treasure. The omens will begin insistently speaking of it and you'll try to ignore them. During the third year, your wife will be unhappy because she'll feel she interrupted your quest. Many days you'll walk the sands of the desert thinking maybe you should have left. And sometime in the fourth year, the omens will abandon you because you stopped listening to them. You'll be dismissed from your position as the tribal counsellor. By then, you'll be a rich merchant with lots of camels. But you'll spend the rest of your days knowing that you didn't pursue your Personal Legend and that now it is too late."

There was no beating around the bush here; he hit him with the straight dope.

The Alchemist's message is relevant to all of us. There is something deep within us urging us forward to pursue our own Personal Legend. It feels terrifying at every step of the pursuit. It's scary when we have nothing to lose, and it's scary when we have everything to lose.

If you build up the cajones to go for it when you really want something, *"the universe conspires in helping you achieve it."* But if you give in to the fear and turn your back on your Personal Legend, then this dream will abandon you. Over time, as you settle for mediocrity, the dreams you had when you were younger will vanish.

Conversations With The Heart

We all have weird senses about things that seem to resonate from deep within. We can decide to palm it off like it's nothing, or we can choose to listen to it intently.

If we listen closely to our heart, we might find that wherever it is pointing is, in fact, the direction of our treasure. If we listen and take heed, we'll never be able to keep it quiet. Our hearts will keep guiding us with hints and messages about life and the future. If you trust your heart, it will treat you to your greatest treasures. It is the one instrument we have that knows about our dreams and how we can pursue them.

Having copped a spray from the other Alchemist, Santiago decided to connect with his heart. He listened so intently that he found the advice he needed.

His heart said:

"People are afraid to pursue their most important dreams because they feel that they don't deserve them or that

they'll be unable to achieve them. Our hearts become fearful of treasures that might have been found that were hidden forever in the sands because when these things happen, we suffer terribly. No heart has ever suffered when it goes in search of its dreams."

When Santiago reflected, he knew it was true. Despite the hiccups along his journey, the successes and failures had one thing in common: every second in pursuit of his treasure had been enlightening. He had discovered things along the way that he would never have otherwise. As he evolved along his journey, he was able to try things that would've seemed impossible in his former life. He certainly wouldn't have had the tenacity required to give it a red-hot crack if he hadn't grown through each setback.

When he was finally ready, once he had finally transformed enough to fulfil his Personal Legend, Santiago went to the pyramids and discovered his treasure.

LESSON 1 | *Vision*

The Alchemist is no doubt a weird book with a message embedded deep within that is hard to interpret. The author Paulo Coelho spent just two weeks writing the entire book. According to Coelho, he could write that fast because the "book was already written in his soul."

Despite being a flop in its first year, barely selling a few hundred books, the universe continued to conspire for Coelho to make it a success. The book went on to sell over 65 million copies! But really, the idea of it being a flop or commercial success was kind of meaningless because Coelho knew he was living out his Personal Legend.

Everyone on Earth has a treasure that awaits them. Yet our hearts seldom say much about the treasures because we no longer search for them. Hearts typically only speak to children. When our hearts feel ignored, when their advice is not listened to or acted upon, they gradually go quiet.

Early in our lives, possibilities are endless. We can entertain all the excitement our futures might have us. But as we stop listening to our hearts, as we stop listening to its advice, our hearts speak softer and softer, to the point of eventually not speaking at all. Why would they bother speaking up when the captain isn't listening to a word they say?

Although this is a fictional story, there are practical lessons we can all take from it:

Firstly, we all have a Personal Legend that, if fulfilled, will lead to a happier, more abundant and less burdensome life.

Secondly, fear will hold us back. We'll be constantly challenged with moments of choice: to follow our heart in the direction of our Personal Legend or stay put and accept mediocrity.

And finally, there is no shortcut to gold. We need to take the necessary steps with the required boldness in order to change ourselves and find our treasure.

CHAPTER 2
Peak Experience

"Most of us are working in infectious fear factories."

Inspired by: **Peak,** *by Chip Conley*

You probably came across Maslow at some stage in high school. I know I (Jonesy) did, but it was tainted by the wankiness that can come from a Year 9 Psychology teacher. Rediscovering his content a little later in life, it turns out his framework is extremely useful. In many ways, these ideas wrap a bit of science around the lessons Santiago learnt intuitively on his path. Maslow's theories shine a light on the journeys we can take to discover our Personal Legend, and reach our highest purpose in life.

Plenty of studies in books are based on poor old lab rats. Throughout the day, a rat will go hungry, face electrocution several times and be thrown into a maze to run around pointlessly until death. A horrible experience, but apparently, most psychologists reckon it is all worth it because of their contribution to behavioural science.

Maslow looked at things differently. We can only learn so much from a starving, electrocuted lab rat. Instead, Maslow looked to humans, specifically focusing on the high achievers. He studied the peak performers across all domains, such as arts and business. And unlike most psychologists of his time, he chose not to analyse how past events may have made us psychologically unhealthy, preferring to focus on the higher ceilings of our potential. By recognising that all humans have a higher nature, Maslow helped spawn the Human Potential Movement in the 1960s and 1970s.

"A musician must make music, an artist must paint, a poet must write, if he is to be ultimately at peace with himself. What a man can be, he must be. We may call this need 'self-actualization'. This tendency might be phrased as the desire to become more and more what one is, to become everything that one is capable of becoming."

- Abraham Maslow

Hierarchy of Needs

The foundation of Maslow's work is his *Hierarchy of Needs*. This presumes that the human being is a perpetually wanting animal that rarely reaches a state of complete satisfaction. When one desire is satisfied, another pops up to take its place. Hence, once one desire is satisfied, it is no longer a motivator of behaviour, and we become driven by something new.

Maslow's pyramid had five groups of needs, which can be grouped together as follows[5]:

- *Basic needs:* These are our physiological needs, so we don't go hungry (food, water, shelter), and our safety needs in order to feel secure.
- *Psychological needs:* These include the feeling of belonging, connection with friends and loved ones, and the feeling of accomplishment.
- *Self-fulfilment:* Living to our full potential.

---

[5] The original five needs (physiological, safety, love/belonging, esteem, self-actualisation) became three needs (basic, psychological, self-fulfilment).

hierarchy of needs.

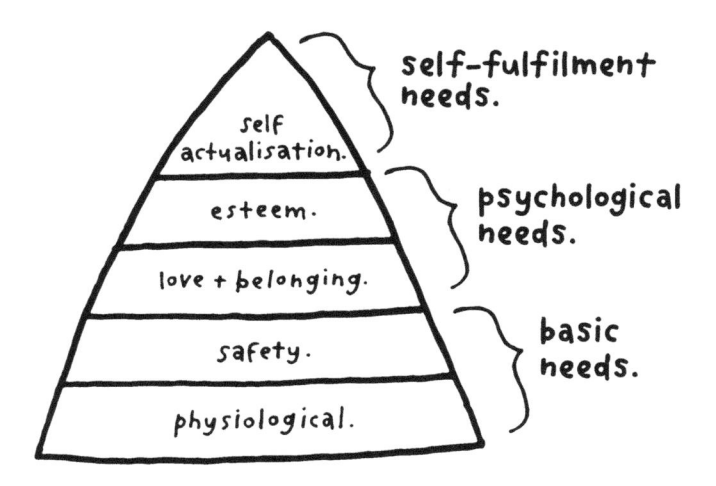

```
        /\
       /self\
      /actualisation.\     } self-fulfilment
     /----------------\      needs.
    /    esteem.       \
   /--------------------\  } psychological
  /   love + belonging.  \    needs.
 /------------------------\
/        safety.           \ } basic
/--------------------------\   needs.
/      physiological.       \
-----------------------------
```

We start at the bottom and work our way up. No point focusing on love and relationships if we don't have food in the fridge. No point in working on activities that could contribute to our self-esteem when we're lacking safety and security.

In order to get the most out of life, we build our way up the pyramid - locking in the base layer first, then building sequentially upon each previously satisfied need until we get to the pointy bit up top. Without the support of the lower foundation, our pyramid will topple.

The Work Pyramid

Maslow's pyramid is broadly applicable across all human activities. One possible application is to link it to the 'work' context.

Let's consider our friend Santiago from the previous chapter:

- Initially, working as a shepherd, he brought in enough money to keep himself warm and keep himself fed. He was meeting his *basic needs*.
- When he moved to the Oasis, he gained status and recognition as a leader, as well as strong relationships, both personal and professional. He was meeting his *psychological needs*.
- Then, when he went to the pyramids (literally), he climbed to the top of Maslow's pyramid (metaphorically). He was following his Personal Legend and achieving his full potential - transforming into gold (metaphorically) by finding gold (literally). He was meeting his *self-fulfilment* needs.

Back in the real world, we can apply this to the workplace and see how an employee can climb the (metaphorical) pyramid, as Santiago did. The three equivalent levels of our "work" pyramid would be: *money, recognition*, and *meaning*. Just like

Maslow's pyramid, we need to climb this work pyramid by achieving needs sequentially in order to start working on the next.

Some not-for-profit organisations may assume the whole employee experience is the sense of *meaning* they get in the workplace. But this is trying to get straight to the top of the pyramid without building a solid foundation. If they aren't getting paid enough *money* to cover rent and groceries, or they're not getting the *recognition* they deserve for doing a good job, employees will never get to the top of the pyramid and can never connect with the *meaning* that may be on offer.

However, most people have the opposite problem. They spend too much time focused on the base of the pyramid. They start their careers hyper-focused on money and financial incentives. If they manage to progress, they get hooked on power and status and *recognition*, never tapping into a true sense of *meaning* and fulfilment.

Job / Career / Calling

Three bricklayers were working on the side of the road. An old lady walking her dog strolled past and asked what they were up to. The first man replied: *"Making a wage."* The second said: *"I am doing the best bricklaying job in the country."* And the final proclaimed: *"I'm building a grand cathedral to spread messages of light and positivity."*

LESSON 1 | *Vision*

The first was operating at the base of the pyramid, focusing on basic needs. People who view their work as a 'job' tend to focus on the financial rewards of working rather than pleasure or fulfilment. The job is for money, and they try and find enjoyment outside of their 9-5 existences.

The second was in the middle of the pyramid, focused on psychological needs (status and recognition). Those who view their work as a 'career' focus primarily on advancement and growing their talent. Whilst they gain some satisfaction from the work itself, their esteem often comes from external sources like a promotion or a raise.

The third man was at the top of the pyramid living out a self-actualised life. Those lucky enough to pursue a 'calling' find meaning and fulfilment through their work, regardless of money or recognition.

How do you know which level you are?

At the *job* level, you might say something like this: *I like what I do, but don't expect much from work. I enjoy my leisure life more than my work life. I'm often not excited about work on a Monday. I consciously use vacation time and sick days to create balance so that work doesn't dominate.*

If you're in a *career*, it goes a little like this: *My greatest experience at work is when I'm recognised by others. My goal in life is to rise to the top of my field. I will do what it takes to become a success in my work.*

LESSON 1 | *Vision*

And if you're following your *calling*, it feels like this: *I tend to lose myself at work. I just feel like I'm in flow and lose a sense of time. My work makes a difference in the world. I feel my work allows me to show the real me.*

It might be a revelation to realise your current work pyramid puts you in the job or career category. If this is the honest truth, it may be time to find a new pyramid, scale it to the top, and tap into your calling.

LESSON 1 | *Vision*

CHAPTER 3
Keys To Fulfilment

"Ignorance is the most expensive thing in the world."

Inspired by: **Life In Half A Second,**
By Matthew Michaelwicz

Life is short.

You know it. We know it. It's cliche.

But how short exactly?

Planet Earth is four and a half *billion* years old. For a loooong time, there wasn't much inhabiting the planet.

Homo Sapiens emerged 'only' about 200,000 years ago. That sounds like a long time, but we say *only* 200,000 years because Homo Sapiens have only been around for about 0.0044% of the planetary time scale.

To put it another way, if the history of the Earth was compressed into just one year, modern humans would have only been here for 23 minutes. And on this time scale, our

LESSON 1 | *Vision*

entire life would amount to half a second. In planet time, that's all we've got. Just *half a second*.

We don't appreciate this when we're young. Time seems unlimited. It just whizzes by, and it seems like infinitely more is coming around the corner. Each year it seems to be moving faster. This isn't such a bad thing when we're impatient to grow up, become adults and join the 'real world.' We envisage all the freedoms we might have. All the things we could do.

But when adulthood arrives, reality kicks in. We discover that this 'freedom' we were waiting for is a bit of a sham. Instead, we're paying bills and surviving in jobs that most of us don't care about.

Life as an adult isn't what we imagined it would be as kids. We've got half a second, and we're spending it doing things that we don't really want to be doing. We hope that maybe something, or someone, might whisk us away and save us from this misery. But that long-awaited saviour never comes, and time seems to keep barrelling forward faster and faster.

Don't get us wrong; the tragedy isn't that we only have half a second. *The real tragedy is that we waste it.*

You are the beneficiary of millions of years of unimaginable good luck. The spinning planet whips together just the right cells in just the right order at just the right temperature and

LESSON 1 | *Vision*

just the right atmospheric pressure to kick off a chain reaction of billions of years of evolution. Hundreds of thousands of generations, with each branch of your ancestral history getting jiggy with it at the right time on the right night for you to win the sperm race against millions of your potential brothers and sisters that didn't quite make it to the egg in time. The odds are so astronomically small that it's not a thousand-to-one shot that you made it here alive or even a trillion-to-one; it's basically infinity-to-one odds.

Now, here we are, with just half a second to enjoy the privilege. And what do we do with that half a second? Everything *other* than what we want!

There's a countdown on our lives. And guess what - there is a countdown on yours too. The shortness of life can be scary... or we can choose to use it as motivation instead. We can choose to do something with our time here and make the most of it. And the only way to make the most of that half a second is by being clear on what we want.

This brings us to the 'five keys to fulfilment.' Successful people *get* what they want out of life because they *know* what they want. They have a specific vision. To achieve success and attain a sense of fulfilment, you must first know what success looks like for you, and then get after it.

Key 1: *Clarity*

You can't stumble yourself to success.

In fact, you *won't* stumble your way to success. Without clarity, without knowing what you want, your life will be an accident. However pleasant or unpleasant, your life will just sort of happen.

Instead, we need to define what 'success' means to us. To define what we want in life, we must define a goal. People don't fail because they set small goals. They fail in life because they don't aim at all. Taking aim and setting a goal has this unique power of getting your brain to filter out all the irrelevant information and concentrate on the essentials.

I (Ashto) was extremely excited to meet my niece in her first week of existence. A few days after she was born, I held her for the first time and expected some kind of deep connection. But all she did was cry and reach out for her mother to get more food. Fortunately for her (but unfortunately for me), the human brain has developed an information filtering system to eliminate the nonsense, like her new uncle's emotional needs. This is known as the Reticular Activating System.

Reticular activation has kept our species alive and away from extinction by allowing us to focus on food sources, mating opportunities, things that are familiar and safe, and

LESSON 1 | *Vision*

things that are potential threats. You'll notice this system kicks into gear after buying a new car. Once upon a time, I won a TV game show[6] and bought my wife a Hyundai Tuscon with the winnings. Previously I had no idea what a Hyundai Tuscon looked like and had never seen one on the road before, but the day after I bought one, suddenly they were everywhere! It's not that Hyundai sold thousands of cars overnight - they'd always been there, I was just noticing them for the first time. That's the Reticular Activation System at work.

This system is what makes setting goals so powerful. In 1987, Jim Carrey was a largely unknown struggling actor. He wrote a cheque addressed to himself for $10,000,000 for "acting services rendered," with a future date of 1994. For years he carried around this cheque in his wallet, even though he didn't have more than a few bucks to his name. He constantly looked at it and dreamt about the possibilities, visualising his future life with 10 mil in the bank. When he was eventually cast for *Dumb and Dumber* in 1994, he was paid... you guessed it - $10,000,000 for acting services rendered.

It took Jim Carrey less than a minute to define his goal on a post-dated check. In the years ahead, this high-leverage moment created a goal that provided him the compass on which to direct his thoughts and actions.

---

[6] Maybe another story for another time.

LESSON 1 | *Vision*

Research shows that out of 100 people:
- 80 don't have goals.
- 16 have goals... but fail to write them down.
- 3 have goals and write them down, but don't review them.
- Only 1 has goals, writes them down, and regularly reviews them.

Defining what we want in life is rather simple. All we need to do is whip out a piece of paper and start writing down what we want. As we learned with Santiago, if you trust yourself and listen to your heart, you might get a clue as to what your Personal Legend might be.

Key 2: *Desire*

No matter how large or small, all decisions stem from *desire*.

Take gardening. Anyone can set up a garden, whether it takes up your whole backyard or a few pots on a window sill. I (Ashto) set up a little veggie patch when I first moved out of home. I planted carrots, broccoli, peas, beetroot, all sorts of stuff. It was exciting at first, seeing the little shoots pop up. But a few weeks later, progress seemed to stall, and I found myself back at the supermarket buying my veggies. Clearly, the desire wasn't strong enough for me to see it through, and the veggie patch quickly filled up with weeds.

The same goes for other goals too. The reason we fail, simply comes down to desire. If we abandon our goal midstream, it is because our desire to achieve the goal is less than the desire to do some other activity instead. The odds of achieving our goals are directly correlated with our desire. If it's red hot, we'll probably succeed. If it's lukewarm, we'll probably fail.

Key 3: *Belief*

Researchers conducted a study on 180 patients requiring knee surgery. Half got the prescribed surgery. The other half got sham surgery where they put them under, sliced open the knee, and then sewed it back up without actually doing anything. The patients had no idea which group they were in as they were all wheeled into the operating theatre, given an anaesthetic, and woke with a wound that needed to heal.

The result? Those who didn't get the actual operation improved just as much as those who did. Weeks later, the people who previously couldn't walk were out there running around and kicking the footy as if their knee was as good as new!

Then there is Roger Bannister, an Oxford student and gifted runner. At the 1952 Olympics, he finished in fourth place, just missing out on a medal. This hurt. But it also gave him a

LESSON 1 | *Vision*

burning desire to do better. The next year he set the goal to be the first man to run a mile in under four minutes. He publicly announced his goal and trained like never before. On May 6th 1954, he recorded an official time of 3:59.3. The title "first person to run a mile in under four minutes" was his.

Bannister achieved his goal with the first two keys: he was clear on what he wanted, and he had the desire to achieve it. But the most interesting part of this story was what happened later. Previously, this mystical "four-minute mile" was just a pipe dream, an asymptote beyond the limits of human ability that would never be achieved. But just six weeks after Bannister showed it could be done, another bloke broke the barrier too. Over the following months and years, dozens of runners from around the world did the same. Today, the four-minute mile is commonplace. You could basically *walk* a mile in four minutes now! [7]

What the hell happened? The human body has the same infrastructure. Only one thing changed over time: *Belief.* Other runners broke the same barrier because now they knew it could be done.

---

[7] OK, it's not quite *that* commonplace... but it's pretty standard for professional middle distance runners. At the time of writing, 1,663 athletes have now achieved the feat that used to be viewed as "impossible".

Key 4: *Knowledge*

Everything is easier if we know how to do it. Say we want to make a million bucks. This would be a nice round number for Jonesy to buy his coveted Tesla and pay off the mortgage.

There are many ways to do it. For example, we might invest $287 per month in the stock market that grows at an average of 8% compounded annually - in 40 years, we'll hit our mil. Or we can give it a shot by starting a business, which might get us there quicker, but with less certainty - we might get there in 10 years, or we might fail. Or, we can take a good old punt - head to the casino with our life savings, and we might be able to double up enough times in a row to get there in just one night (if we don't bust first).

Each path has its own nuances and its unique advantages and disadvantages. Knowledge is about understanding all options - the risks and rewards of each potential pathway. Getting to any goal is infinitely easier once we know *how*.

LESSON 1 | *Vision*

Key 5: *Action*

As one of our mutual friends and golf coach/life coach/business coach/social media coach/coach coaching coaches how to coach once said: *"Do or do not... there is no try."*

Reading this book won't deliver you a good attitude. You must read books, then *take action*[8]. Attending wealth seminars won't make you wealthy. You must attend the seminars and then *take action*.

If you sit on your ass and do nothing... then nothing will happen. Without action, the first four keys to fulfilment are useless.

---

[8] Or, as became our go-to answer when people interview us on their podcast and ask us to give their audience our best piece of advice: *"Read books and do shit"*.

Lesson 2

change.

LESSON 2 | *Change*

Change is inevitable. It is our attitude toward change that will inform whether we experience fear or a deep excitement for what is to come.

Let's take the metaphor of a river: constantly flowing, constantly changing. We can choose to pretend that change doesn't exist and adopt the attitude of a rock, stuck at the bottom, watching the world around us fly by. While it might be comfortable and cosy nestled on a bed of sand, we become incapable of going with the flow and will inevitably be left behind.

Better, perhaps, is to be like a log. As a log, we are in motion. Cruising along the surface of the river, heading toward a destination. However, if we adopt the attitude of a log, our experience may be chaotic as we are pushed around by currents along our journey and swept into banks without any agency over where we end up.

Which leads us to the kayaker. When it comes to change, adopting the attitude of a kayaker is the power move. In this position, we ride the river with much greater control over which way we turn and move. We can go with the flow, steer left or right, turn and battle against the current, ride the rapids, or even pull off to the side and take a breather.

With this attitude, we embrace change and can even relish in the excitement of the ride, while finding we have much greater control over our destination.

LESSON 2 | *Change*

CHAPTER 4
The Beach Bum and The Millionaire

"Any time you see what looks like a breakthrough, it is always the end result of a long series of little things, done consistently over time."

Inspired by: **The Slight Edge,** *by Jeff Olson*

There were two lads from New Mexico. Both went to school together, graduated together, and became college roommates. Both were pretty personable guys; they had similar upbringings, and they were both mischief-makers. When you add it all up in terms of skills and potential, they were evenly matched - almost identical in every way.

The first friend dropped out of college and moved to Florida. He became a beach bum: he lifted weights, chased girls, and let his blond hair grow long and curly. People started calling him Gorgeous George as he looked like the WWE wrestler of the same name. He worked at a golf course

LESSON 2 | Change

to make ends meet, lugging around heavy golf bags for rich people, but ultimately, he had no vision.

Then there was Gorgeous George's buddy. As an adult, this guy lived a charmed life. He went through college with straight A's before enrolling in business school and graduating at the top of his class. He was recruited by a gigantic tech firm, built a stellar resume, and went on to create a string of successful entrepreneurial ventures. Today his life is rich in every way, with an amazing daughter, friends around the globe, and a record-breaking business.

Due to their childhood friendship, the millionaire stays in very close contact with the beach bum. He knows that he could have taken either life path - he could've become a millionaire, or he could've been just like the beach bum. As a matter of fact, he was.

The reason they were roommates all those years and shared the same upbringing is because they are *the same person*. At different points in his life, Jeff Olson was both the beach bum *and* the millionaire.

Olson has had a lot of success in life, but it wasn't always the case. He started out as Gorgeous George, the college dropout golf caddy. There was no enlightenment, no near-death experience, no lightning strike that led to overnight change - in fact, he's still that same guy. He didn't change who he was as much as he changed what he *did*.

The difference between these two contrasting lives can be defined by one thing: the *Slight Edge*. You too can follow this path to transition from where you are now to where you want to be.

Two Graphs

The Oscillating Wave

When it comes to success, people generally tend to ride the rollercoaster. When they find themselves in a rut, they work hard to climb back up the hill. But once things start looking okay again, they ease their foot off the pedal, begin to coast, and ultimately settle with how things are. Before long, the bad habits creep back in, and they start going over the edge of the rollercoaster back down to the next lull.

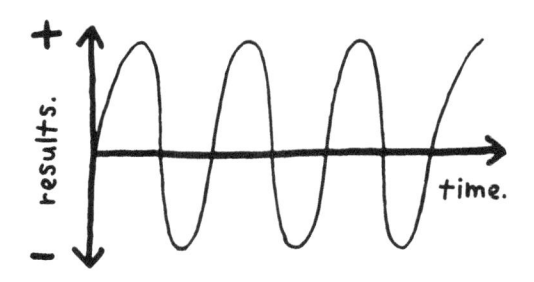

the oscillating wave.

LESSON 2 | *Change*

The Slight Edge

Most people oscillate between survival and failure, survival and failure. But the *really* successful people are the ones that tap into that upward momentum, hit the top of the wave... then keep going!

They work out what changes got them to the top, and instead of reverting to their old ways and heading back down the slippery slope to failure, they keep at them. They keep changing and keep improving.

the slight edge.

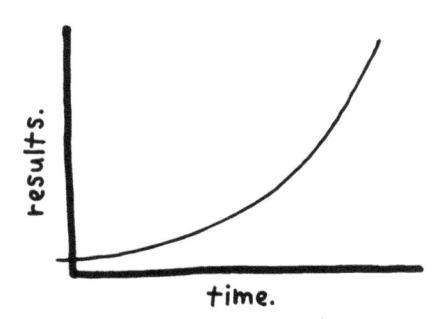

[Graph: results vs. time showing an exponential curve]

It makes complete sense - if we keep doing the things that got us from failure to survival in the first place (the things we clearly know how to do since we're already doing them), they would eventually carry us all the way to success.

What are those things? What are the actions that take us up that curve? And what are the actions dragging us down that we need to avoid?

One word: *simple*. The things that take us out of failure and up toward survival and then on to success are simple. They are so simple, in fact, that it's easy to overlook them. They seem insignificant. They're not sweeping gestures that take a huge effort. Just little things we can do every day that nobody else even notices.

They are things that are simple to do, yet only successful people actually do them. Unsuccessful people know about them but do nothing:

- Put a few bucks from each paycheck into savings
- Read ten pages of a book
- Do a few minutes of exercise throughout the day
- Go for a walk around the block each afternoon
- Take a moment to tell someone you appreciate them

These little things could seem kind of pointless, but if done consistently every day, they compound over time to yield enormous results. *Simple productive actions repeated consistently over time.* That, in a nutshell, is the Slight Edge.

The Cost of Waiting

There was once a little water plant with a big dream. Growing near the edge of a sizeable pond, the water hyacinth wondered what it was like on the other side of the pond. But the pond just laughed in its face: *"You think you, a tiny little water lily that can't move, can ever grow big enough to see the other side*

LESSON 2 | *Change*

of the pond? Impossible." But what the pond didn't know was that the water hyacinth could change.

Each plant produces around 5,000 seeds - it grows not by moving or spreading out but by doubling itself. On the first day, it was just a single little flower. On the second day, it doubled. But even still, two little flowers tucked to the edge of the water weren't concerning the pond. Then it doubled again on the third, fourth, and fifth days. By day 15, after 15 doublings, it barely covered a square foot of the water. The pond again laughed at the measly little thing. By day 20, it had finally grown enough that someone walking past the pond would notice a small patch of flowers. On day 29, half the pond was covered, and on day 30, the water hyacinth achieved its vision of reaching the other side.

You've probably heard a story about compound interest like this before. Whether it's a penny turning into a million bucks, a tree growing from a seed to a forest, or a single flower growing to cover an entire pond. Compound interest is a powerful story... but it's useless unless you act on it.

You see, the Slight Edge is already working, right now. It's been building momentum your whole life. It's either working *for* you... or *against* you. If we're not actively harnessing the power of the Slight Edge, if we're not consistently doing those small productive things, the power of compound interest might be gaining steam in the wrong direction. That cheeky donut after dinner won't matter much today, but if you have a donut a day for five years, we'll start to see the impact. Scrolling on our phones instead of reading a book for ten minutes doesn't change much right now, but the accumulation of decades of forgone knowledge means we'll find ourselves miles from where we could have been.

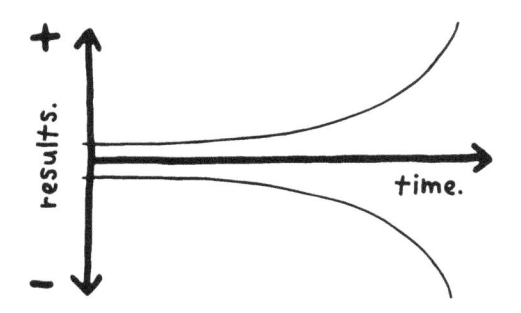

[Figure: a graph with "results." on the vertical axis (+ up, − down) and "time." on the horizontal axis, showing two curves diverging away from zero — one upward and one downward — over time.]

The Slight Edge is relentless - it cuts both ways. Productively harnessed, it carries us towards success. Carelessly overlooked, it drags us towards failure.

The truth is, everything is curved. There are no straight lines in life. Everything is constantly changing. It feels like today is much the same as yesterday, and tomorrow probably won't be much different either. But those ever-so-slight differences, the ones we can't really perceive - they're there. And they're adding up.

If you remember back to high school mathematics, you'll know that exponential curves are basically flat for a long time... then seemingly out of nowhere, they take off.

LESSON 2 | *Change*

Compound interest and the Slight Edge are exponential curves. You might feel as though your life path is a straight line, but it's subtly curving either up or down. Way off in the distance, something is going to happen. We're either going to rocket upwards, or we're about to drop off a cliff. It all comes down to those little, seemingly insignificant, daily actions.

Up or down. The choice is yours.

- *Health:* What exercise are you doing each day? What are you putting in your cakehole[9]? Are you feeling stronger every day, or like you're slowly deteriorating?
- *Happiness:* Are you grateful for the people you have around you? Do you savour the little moments? Are you content in today's present rather than reliving yesterday's past or stressing about tomorrow's future? Are you building toward greater happiness and fulfilment or sinking deeper into unhappiness and dissatisfaction?
- *Relationships:* Do you have mutually enriching friendships? Are you cultivating connection, or are you slowly drifting apart? Are your relationships growing deeper and richer or becoming stale and distant?
- *Personal development:* Are you gradually building knowledge, or is it slowly eroding? Are you learning more and more about the truths of life or sinking deeper and deeper into denial?

---

[9] Hopefully, actual cake goes into your cakehole, but only occasionally. Calling it a "kalehole" doesn't have the same ring to it.

- *Finances:* Are you building toward a long-term plan, or are you fuelled by credit and going deeper into the red? Are you establishing long-term foundations and security or eroding it?
- *Career:* Are you building skills and developing your reputation, or drifting further and further behind your potential? Is your professional value improving or diminishing?
- *Impact:* How will people remember you when you're gone? As someone who produced and contributed, or as someone who just took?

Life is not a practice session. There is no rehearsal. This is it.

The good news is that every day we have a choice. The choice we make today determines where we'll be in 10, 20 or 50 years from now. Are we stepping on the path that's gradually curving downward, or are we grabbing hold of the Slight Edge and making it work in our favour?

Right now, in the present, our future is stretching out in front of us. For as far as we can see, it probably looks like both paths are the same. But the further we move into the future, the greater the gap between the two paths. By choosing those small, positive daily actions, we're putting ourselves on the best possible trajectory.

LESSON 2 | *Change*

A few small, simple, daily changes might be all it takes to help you achieve your vision.

Is it easy to make those tiny changes? Abso-bloody-lutely it is.

Is it easy not to? Tragically so.

CHAPTER 5
Overcoming Obstacles To Change

"Transformative behaviour change is more like treating a chronic disease than curing a rash."

Inspired by: **How To Change,** *by Katy Milkman*

I (Jonesy) went to the dentist for the first time in a long time. Whilst the dentist was jovial at the start, as soon as I opened up my gob, he started giving me a hard time. The last time I'd seen him, he'd told me: *"Get flossing, or you'll be in a bit of trouble when I see you again in 12 months."* Well, I didn't see him 12 months later; it was actually four and a half years later, and surprise surprise... there was still 99.8m of floss left in the 100m Colgate bulk pack I'd bought. I reckon I must've used it once the first night I bought it, then never again. What was meant to be a simple check-up and clean turned out to be a real ordeal. Every time the dentist got near my gums,

LESSON 2 | *Change*

they started bleeding. By the end of the session, I felt like I'd swallowed about a pint of my own blood.

I want to floss. I really do! But I can't think of anything more boring than spending two minutes every day doing something as seemingly inconsequential as pulling a measly piece of string back and forth.

I know it, you know it. Change can be bloody hard[10].

I bet you've also tried to change before and have encountered how difficult it can be. We can't blame a lack of information. Whether you want to build your retirement savings, read more, exercise more, eat healthier... there are plenty of books, workshops, TED Talks, coaches and gurus that all claim to have the answer. You've probably even tested a few of the tactics they espouse. Maybe it was skipping coffees, or an intricate system of calendar reminders and alarms, tracking your steps, or weighing yourself every day.

Yet despite all this information and all these attempts, you still haven't made the changes you want...

Why is that? We want to change, and we have a bunch of tips and tricks to help us do it, but something still stands in our way.

---

[10] I still haven't flossed. My dentist is going to really slap me up at the next 'annual' visit in another four and a half years.

One reason is that change is hard - there's no denying that. It's much easier to take the comfortable, easy route and keep things just the way they are.

But a more useful answer is that we haven't yet found the right strategy for this specific change because we haven't identified exactly what hurdles are blocking our path. We take generic advice and try to apply it to our specific problem, but in order to have the best chance at success, it's important that we work out exactly what obstacle we're facing and employ techniques specifically designed to overcome it.

Having read the previous chapter, you now know the upside of changing. By making small, positive changes, we're stepping off that downward slope and taking advantage of the Slight Edge. The question now is not *"should* I change?" but *"how* do I change?"

Let's dive into three obstacles to change and look at how we can overcome them.

Obstacle #1: *Laziness*

In Germany, the rate of organ donation is 15%. That is, 15% of adults in Germany are officially registered and have granted permission to donate their organs after they die. Their next-door neighbour, Austria, a seemingly similar country

LESSON 2 | *Change*

(language, culture, geographic region, ethnicity, etc.), has over 90% registered organ donors. How the hell can that be? Are we talking about the same species of humans?

The difference between these two neighbouring countries is that Germany's organ donation policy is "opt-in," whereas Austria's is "opt-out." If you want to donate your organs in Germany, you have to go and fill out the paperwork, get it signed by some recognised authority, and go through a few weeks of waiting and processing in order to get on the list. In Austria, you're automatically assumed to be an organ donor, and the only time you need to fill out any forms is if you want to *remove* yourself from the list.

Australia is also an opt-in system for organ donation. We've both sat through presentations at work from the Australian Organ Donor Register, we've heard the stories of people whose lives were saved thanks to an organ donor, we've seen videos of parents overcome with emotion for a generous dead person who gave their son or daughter a second chance at life. We've both been convinced that we probably won't need our organs when we kick the bucket and that someone else might really benefit from them. We've got the flyers and pamphlets; we've even got the forms we need to join up. Yet still, neither of us are organ donors... not because we don't want to, but because we're lazy.

LESSON 2 | *Change*

One of the big barriers to change is *laziness*. We're passive; we go with the flow, and we take the easy road. In general, this is a good thing - it helps us save wasted effort and conserve energy by *not* doing things that don't need to be done. But there are downsides to going with the flow too. Laziness makes change hard. We want to cook a healthy meal, but laziness takes over, and we order Uber Eats. We want to read a book before bed, but laziness takes over, and we chuck on Netflix. We want to go for a run, but laziness takes over, and we get stuck in an Instagram infinite scroll. Laziness leads us toward our default options.

Thankfully, we can turn this tendency into a solution. If we want to make a change, the easiest way is to change our default settings. If we make our 'go to' easy option a good thing, we'll be well on our way to achieving our vision.

In some cases, changing the default is like changing from an "opt-in" system to an "opt-out" system and seeing a 6X improvement in organ donation rates. Usually, though, it requires a bit more work. Going for the apple instead of going for the chocolate bar might take a week of training, going for a run instead of going for the couch might take a month, and going for a book instead of going for the TV might take a year. But while it can be initially hard to change these habits[11],

---

[11] If you want to dive deeper into how you can break old habits or form new ones, check out our book *The Sh*t They Never Taught You* and head to Lesson 3: *Programming The Autopilot*.

once we've put in the work to alter our default setting, we can cruise on autopilot.

Installing new habits is like putting ourselves in "set and forget" mode - we no longer need to think about change, and we no longer need to fight laziness... laziness actually helps us stay on track because we've programmed a new setting that we're going to default to! You will have put yourself on the Slight Edge path, so now change happens automatically.

Obstacle #2: *Impulsivity*

In 2009, a team of Volkswagen technicians snuck into a Swedish train station in the middle of the night to do something a little unusual. No, they weren't setting up a car display (how the hell do they get cars into the middle of shopping centres and airports anyway?!); they were transforming a regular old set of stairs into a giant piano.

The team set up a video camera to capture how people changed. The day before, when it was just regular steps, most people took the escalator right next to it. Makes sense - why walk up the steps when you can be carried by a machine? There was the occasional weirdo that took the stairs instead of the escalator, but the vast majority went the easier path to the top.

Then, on the day the piano stairs randomly appeared, everyone was using the stairs. It didn't matter if you were

LESSON 2 | *Change*

a businesswoman on the way to an important meeting, a schoolkid on your way to class, or even a dog going for a walk around the city - the piano stairs were so fun that everyone had a go[12]. Some people played scales using both the black and the white keys, some people tried to perform duets, some ran up and down multiple times, and others just thought it was funny. It was the reverse of the day before: instead of a packed escalator and the occasional oddball taking the stairs, now the stairs were chocker-block, and only a few weirdos went for the escalator.

We're impulsive as a species. We chase the shiny new object, we go for the quick fix instead of the long hard slog, and we opt for fun over boring. This is not a bad thing, but often the changes we want to make aren't inherently exciting. Our impulsivity drives us towards video games instead of exercise or lollies instead of nuts. To overcome the obstacle of impulsivity that can block us from change, we need to find ways to inject a little enjoyment into our desired activities.

9% of premature deaths are caused by insufficient exercise, so taking a few flights of stairs each day can make a surprising difference to our health. It's probably not feasible to turn every staircase in the world into a piano, but there is an important lesson we can learn from this little experiment:

---

[12] Check out the YouTube video, search for *"Piano Stairs - Odenplan, Stockholm, Sweden"* or go to www.youtube.com/watch?v=ipMib6ejGuo

if we want to make a change, the easiest way is to make it fun.

As a wise philosopher once said: *"A spoonful of sugar makes the medicine go down."* Mary Poppins knew that linking something unenjoyable to something sweet was the key to success. The things that are good for us in the long term are usually unenjoyable in the short term (exercise, eating broccoli, practising a new instrument when you suck at it). And the things that are bad for us in the long term feel great in the short term (burgers, ice cream, sitting in the nice warm bean bag in front of the fire instead of going for a swim in the cold ocean).

I (Jonesy) found it difficult to cram exercise in on the weekends. Then I discovered a human-built wave park that pumps out artificial waves. Once I started doing this on Sundays, exercise wasn't so hard. The wave park turned out to be the highlight of my week. And best of all, given my limited ability at surfing, it was also my hardest workout for the week.

By linking some kind of short-term reward to the things that are going to be good for us in the long run, we're far more likely to make the change we desire.

Obstacle #3: *Inertia*

We've spoken about overcoming laziness by changing our default settings and overcoming impulsivity by making it fun; now, we need to overcome inertia by just getting started.

LESSON 2 | *Change*

Inertia is the force that keeps us on the well-worn path, doing the things we've always been doing (or, in many cases, not doing things we know we should). Once we've carved a bit of a groove, it's easy to keep going and stick to the status quo, even if that groove isn't harnessing the Slight Edge.

In order to get started and make our change, we need to pull ourselves out of that old groove and start carving a new one. Once we have set the new changes in place and committed to starting, the power of inertia will keep us on track. The key here isn't about *how* you start but *when* you start. Timing can make all the difference in creating a new groove.

We've all had that "New Year, New Me" moment (or cringed behind someone's back when they boldly announced their grand plans for the year ahead, knowing it would, at best, last a week, if that). While many New Year's Resolutions don't stick, the theory is sound. The 1st of January, while a rather arbitrary day in the history of the world if you didn't have access to a Gregorian calendar, is a great time to wipe the slate clean. It's a day on which we can mentally draw a line between "old me" and "new me." All the bad shit we did was in the past; we magically get to erase it. Old You would be going out to pubs and parties, getting smashed every weekend, losing hours of sleep and days of productivity. New You will be much more sensible and keep it to only every second weekend... or maybe you can aim higher than that. Old You ate a block of chocolate after dinner; New You is going to drink peppermint tea instead. Old You sat at their desk all day; New You is going to go for a walk at lunchtime. January 1st is a chance to start fresh, wipe the slate clean and begin again.

This "blank slate" effect is strong on January 1st every year. But if we're waiting for the First of Jan before starting that new diet or exercise regime, or time management system, we might be waiting a long time. Thankfully, we don't have to wait that long to harness the power of the "fresh start." We can start fresh on the first of *next* month. If that's still too far away, we can start fresh on Monday - that's only a couple of days from now! Other calendar-based fresh start opportunities include a birthday or major national holidays.

Then there are non-date-based fresh starts that are more to do with life milestones. Starting a new course, changing jobs, moving homes, buying a pet, having a child, getting your driver's licence. These are all major transitions in your life that shift the way you view yourself. Going from a student to a worker, or an adult to a parent, or from living at home to living out of home - these are all pivotal points in our lives where we redefine a lot of things (what we do, how others view us, and how we view ourselves).

One study found that 36% of successful attempts at major change - such as ending a personal relationship, starting a new diet or shifting careers - came after moving house (compared to just 13% of unsuccessful ones). Pattern disruptions like these are a great way to shake us out of our old ways, get us out of our old grooves, and start to carve new pathways instead. Since we have this opportunity at a fresh start, we can channel inertia to work for us, not against us, and really dig into those changes we've been putting off for weeks, months, or even years.

Curing The Disease

Achieving transformative behaviour change is more like treating a chronic disease than curing a rash. We can't just slap a little ointment on it and expect it to clear up forever. The internal obstacles that stand in the way of change are akin to the symptoms of a chronic disease. When we diagnose someone with diabetes, we don't give them a single dose of insulin and expect them to be cured... doctors recognise that chronic diseases might require a lifetime of treatment. The same goes for behaviour change: the obstacles to change don't go away the first time we attempt to "treat" them; they require constant vigilance if we want to make your change stick.

Thankfully, *maintaining* change is far easier than *initiating* it. Once we get the ball rolling toward change, it's much easier to *keep* it rolling. By diagnosing these internal obstacles you

LESSON 2 | *Change*

face and consistently using solutions to help overcome them, you'll be well on the way to achieving your vision.

LESSON 2 | *Change*

CHAPTER 6
Making Diamonds

"It is much better to make friends with what you do not know than with what you do know, as there is an infinite supply of the former but a finite stock of the latter."

Inspired by: **Beyond Order,** *by Jordan Peterson*

When coal is subjected to intense heat and pressure, far below the Earth's surface, its atoms rearrange themselves into a perfect repeating crystalline alignment. Under the right conditions, an ugly lump of coal transforms into a beautiful diamond. Diamonds are the hardest substance on Earth, they're extremely durable, and they reflect light. These qualities (strength, durability and shininess) make diamonds valuable. Coal and diamonds are both made of the same substance - they're both different formations of carbon. Heat and pressure transform the base matter of common coal into the crystalline perfection and rare value of the diamond.

The same can be said of a person.

Under Pressure

Jordan Peterson launched his book *12 Rules For Life* in 2018[13]. He sold heaps of copies, so he milked the cash cow a little further in 2021 with *Beyond Order: 12 More Rules For Life*. Rule 7 uses the change that carbon undergoes when subjected to intense pressure as a metaphor for how we can change ourselves.

There are so many forces that dictate our behaviour, pulling our souls in all sorts of directions. These forces are rarely aligned, meaning we do the things we wish we would *not* do and we don't do the things we wish we would.

Most of the time, we are directionless. We're confused. We're paralysed by indecision. Various impulses pull us this way and that; we jump on fads, waste time, procrastinate, and take the comfortable path, which tends to lead us to nowhere in particular. Even though we've clearly started our vision, temptations yank us off course.

We feel terrible about it... yet still, we do not change. This is why our ancestors believed the human soul had ghosts lurking inside of us that sent us veering off course. Whenever we wanted to do one thing, we ended up doing the opposite - so ancient civilisations assumed there must have been some evil demon haunting us that didn't have our best interests at heart.

---

[13] Part IX, Lesson 30, Chapter 108 of the original *The Sh*t They Never Taught You*.

LESSON 2 | *Change*

Thousands of years ago, our options were somewhat limited. Most of us were roaming around looking for a buffalo to bring home for dinner or collecting berries. A few centuries later, we'd be ploughing the fields or harvesting grain. But then, as society developed, options started to open up. There were enough farmers, butchers, and bakers to take care of food for the village, so we had the freedom to be a builder or a blacksmith or a sculptor. Soon we could be an explorer, a painter or a playwright. Today, we can add a software developer, social media influencer, or a scuba diva pizza delivery person[14] into the mix too.

We don't claim to know what's coming next, but we can assure you that whatever the future holds for us, there will be *more* options, not less. As the world becomes more complex, with an ever-increasing number of potential life paths, choosing what we want to do becomes trickier. We can be anything we want in the world, so why the hell settle for just one thing?!

But the inability to decide between 10 different things is the same as being tormented by them all. Without a clear, well-defined vision and non-contradictory goals, it can be difficult to achieve a sense of excitement and enthusiasm that makes life worthwhile.

Shut the door on the options and make the call. When we have a clear vision on a narrow path, we simplify the world.

---

[14] Legit. Google it.

LESSON 2 | *Change*

By shutting off a few potential pathways and closing the door on a whole bunch of options, we're reducing uncertainty, reducing anxiety, reducing shame, and reducing stress. A directionless person is volatile - someone with a vision is at least headed *somewhere*.

Decide.

Aim.

Shoot.

Picking goals and choosing a direction is part of maturation and discipline. If we aim at nothing, we become plagued by everything. If we aim at nothing, we have nowhere to go, nothing to do, and nothing of value in our lives. Value comes from committing to something, making changes towards that vision, and achieving things that other people without our discipline and focus cannot. Value requires the ranking of options and requires sacrificing the lower for the higher.

People like to say: *"You can be anything you want to be"* - but that is too much! *"Anything you want"* is impossible to juggle with the limited time you have... A less inspiring but more accurate statement is: *"You can be something."* We won't see that on too many bumper stickers or daily affirmation Instagram pages, but it's far better to aim for *something* and actually become it than try to be *anything* and become paralysed by choice, never making progress in any direction.

Pick something specific, then go and do it. This means sacrificing a whole lot of "anythings," but the relief and clarity a decision brings can unlock the door to real change.

Commitment Leads To Change

When Peterson was in graduate school studying for his PhD, he found that the courses were a bit shit, the teachers were a bit shit, and the work was a bit shit. People at the beginning of the program were immature and confused.

As they progressed, did more vigorous research, and started planning their long-ass thesis, their character improved. Compared to the freshmen, he noticed a profound improvement in character in everyone who progressed into the more difficult 5th and 6th years of the program. They had better social skills. They became more articulate. They were more disciplined and organised. They had more fun.

To write a thesis that long, sophisticated, and coherent... the *people writing it* had to change into someone more complex, sophisticated and coherent.

Later, when Peterson became a professor, he began mentoring various students. He saw that those who took on extra responsibilities *outside* of the classroom tended to do better *in* the classroom too. Those that did extracurricular activities obtained better grades than those who took the easy path and just did the bare minimum in order to scrape by.

You might think that playing a team sport or taking on an internship, or volunteering to conduct additional lab research would mean you have less time available to commit to studying; hence your grades would suffer. But the opposite was true: those who became more deeply invested in their work and research developed a greater interest in the topics and were forced to become more efficient with their study time - and scored better as a result. Those students who chose not to invest stayed sitting on the surface, stuck as lumps of coal. In comparison, the ones diving deep and purposefully, subjecting themselves to more heat and pressure, were slowly turning into diamonds.

Later still, in his work as a clinical psychologist, Peterson's advice to people in times of uncertainty was always to take the best path available to them *right now*. Patients often came in with lofty ambitions, but these were usually beyond the current realm of possibility and were just a mechanism to avoid real, immediate change. Focusing on the path in front of us generally involves some kind of sacrifice and sometimes means a hit to our ego or a temporary decrease in ambition, but it can set us up for greater success later. It means instead of dreaming of A and B and C and Q and Z, we just pick A and get to work. We can still get to Q and Z, just not yet. By committing to A, and working as hard as possible at it, we'll develop skills and character along the way. Getting really good at A will help us be better at B - if we follow the natural progression, keep working hard, and keep changing and improving when we eventually get to Z, we'll be well-positioned to nail it.

By knuckling down and working as hard as possible on one thing, we're putting ourselves under that immense heat and pressure required to change our underlying structure and transform into diamonds.

It might sound a little counter-intuitive, but by committing to one thing, you'll see the benefits ripple out to all other areas. By taking the harder path, the path of heat and pressure, you become someone who actually *does* something, not just someone who *thinks* and *talks* and *dreams* about doing everything. By simply choosing and committing to work hard towards change in a few specific areas, everything in your life will get better.

LESSON 2 | *Change*

Is There Anything Worth Committing To?

Ultimately, there are two approaches we can take. The first is the attitude of: *"There's nothing worth committing to yet, so I'll sit back and keep looking."*

Where will that lead you? Nowhere.

What will that get you? A whole lot of nothing.

The other attitude we can adopt is: *"I'll pick something to commit to now, whatever it is, and give it my all - then see what happens."* Committing to making a positive change means time and effort - it means taking the harder path of heat and pressure rather than the easier path of comfort and status quo. But commitments bring with them all sorts of benefits: character, love, friendship, skills, connections, and career.

Our choices won't be perfect. We would've likely got just as much satisfaction (or perhaps more) if we'd made a different choice - a different career, a different partner, a different group of friends. But the act of making a choice, committing to it, and working as hard as we possibly can to make it work, brings a whole new level of satisfaction we otherwise couldn't imagine.

People who do not choose become unmoored - they just drift. They float along the surface of their job, stuck at entry level because they never went deep and committed to building skills and getting good. They float along the surface of their

LESSON 2 | *Change*

romantic relationships because they never commit to taking on the good, the bad and the ugly in order to reach a special place of connection. They float along the surface of their friendship groups, never forging those unbreakable bonds that can only come from dialling up the heat and the pressure.

If we set out to make a change (of any kind) and stick to it, we'll be far better off. The benefit of making the commitment to this change will soak into all areas of life. Not only will we find initial success and move closer to our vision, but we will become the *type of person* capable of making positive changes that are internally driven.

This evolution is like the metaphor we laid out at the start of this lesson. You'll no longer be that rock stuck at the bottom of the river or even the log floating along the surface - you'll become the kayaker with the power to control your own journey.

This transformation means your capacity to pick a target, take aim, and start shooting becomes limitless. You might miss a few times. You might miss by *a lot* at first. But if you stick to it, keep learning, and keep refining your aim, you'll get closer and closer. Soon, you'll hit that bullseye.

By embracing change and throwing your determination and energy at just one thing, you are opening the door to endless opportunities. You will start to become something

LESSON 2 | *Change*

instead of the clamouring multitude of nothingness you once were. Change takes practice, and the more you embrace it, the better you'll become at making things happen. Work as hard as you can on at least one thing - it won't take long before you become that rare and valuable diamond.

Lesson 3

learning.

LESSON 3 | *Learning*

If you've ever watched *Survivor*, you'll know there are two ways to start a fire.

One way is to just go for it. Rub two sticks together as hard and fast as physically possible - full bore, hammer-and-tong, sink or swim, do or die, succeed or fail! Throwing everything you have at the challenge in the hope of getting that spark. Normally the biggest, strongest guy in the tribe opts for this approach, thinking brute force is the answer. But they quickly gas out.

When the first bloke is almost passed out on the beach, gasping for air, someone a little more clever will come along and have a go. This person doesn't use their brawn to start the fire; they use their brains. They understand it is more about techniques and tactics than muscle. They make a little notch in the wood, they have their kindling teepee set up, and their coconut husk is prepared and ready to drop in.

And what do you know? While the big bloke is still catching his breath, the tribe is eating their first batch of rice.

Learning a new skill is much the same. An initial burst of enthusiasm is going to help - that do-or-die attitude can propel you through the initial phases of tumbling and stumbling. But having a plan and a formula for learning will keep you going long after you're puffed and exhausted. By trying new things in the right way, with the right attitude, you can avoid a lot of the common pitfalls and accelerate your path toward reaching your vision.

LESSON 3 | *Learning*

CHAPTER 7
Meta-Learning

"It is possible to become world-class in just about anything in six months or less."

Inspired by: **The Four Hour Chef,** *by Tim Ferriss*

As kids, learning comes naturally. We are exposed to so many new things that we're not afraid to have a crack and struggle along the way. As we grow older, many of us seem to close the book on learning. But doing so holds us back from making change and moving toward our vision. So, if we're armed with the right framework and the right attitude, we can rapidly learn new skills and unlock parts of ourselves we never knew existed.

If we want to achieve things we previously thought were miracles, then our approach to learning needs to be *effective*. When learning effectively, we can narrow down the potential learning material to the most important information that comes up at the highest frequency. This reduces the amount we need to learn (and hence the time it takes).

LESSON 3 | *Learning*

Our approach also needs to be *sustainable*. Going back to the fire analogy, Jonesy likes to use 'cheat sticks' in his fireplace - little super flammable chemical things that do all of the work for him. Using these cheat sticks to ignite all the husks will no doubt produce a flame, but if not tended to properly, it will quickly die. If our approach to learning is that of the cheat stick, we'll be left with nothing but the ashes of the skill we once dreamed of learning. Instead, the sustainable method to begin learning is to create a schedule that allows us to stick to it until we can honestly say that we've learnt a new skill.

Whether you want to learn Spanish, Swimming or Sweet Talking (or anything in between), Tim Ferriss's four-step DSSS model is your gateway to getting it done. Using this framework, it is possible to become world-class at anything you like in 6-12 months... maybe even 6-12 weeks.

Deconstruction

Imagine attempting to learn how to play soccer by reading a book. The first year or two of learning would be spent memorising theories, learning the different techniques for different types of shots, and trying to understand all of the rules... without ever going out onto a field or even touching a ball.

The first problem is that you'd probably give up long before the point where you played a game - without the

LESSON 3 | *Learning*

fun of actually *doing* the thing you're trying to learn, you'd completely lose interest. You'd put the books away and never think about soccer again.

The second problem is that if you ever did make it out onto the pitch and first try to kick a ball, you'd be awful! In your brain, you will have all of the knowledge there is, you'll have the perfect image of what a skilled soccer player should look like... and you'll be far from it. Paper knowledge is one thing, but turning it into practical skill is a whole different beast. There will be such a mismatch between brain and body that you'll scurry home crying and never want to look at a soccer ball again.

Instead, if we actually want to learn some kind of real-world skill, we need to find a way of practising it in the real world as soon as possible. Some initial research is always smart: reading some books or articles, watching some videos, speaking to someone who is already good at that skill - these things can help accelerate us through those initial stages and help avoid wasting time learning things we won't actually ever need to learn. But too much time researching and not enough time practising is a recipe for disaster.

If you want to learn to play the piano, by all means, start learning a little bit of basic music theory, but on your first practice session, ensure you learn to play *Hot Crossed Buns* or *Three Blind Mice* (or, my (Ashto's) grandmother would hate

LESSON 3 | *Learning*

me saying this, even *Chopsticks*[15]). These little wins will keep you engaged early on when you inevitably suck.

The best way to actually learn something in the real world, without getting overwhelmed and/or giving up, is to first and foremost answer this question: *"How do I break this amorphous skill into small, manageable pieces?"*

After I (Ashto) had become a little obsessed with learning to play golf for a year, my mum wanted to come with me and give it a shot herself. After about 15 air swipes, she finally said: *"How do you actually HIT this bloody thing?!"* It's surprising and amazing (and frustrating) how hard it is to hit a ball that is literally just sitting there. You could understand if you couldn't connect with a cricket ball - you've got someone bowling it really fast, with variable bounce, and sometimes with swing or spin. But in golf, the ball doesn't move... you've got a large stick and a small ball, and it's really bloody hard just to make a connection.

If you want to "learn to play golf," you could just go and play a round of 9 or 18 holes at a course. But you'll definitely suck. You'll be lucky to hit it straight if you hit it at all. A

---

[15] This is her least favourite song, and she would kick you out of the house if you played it on her piano. I got one back at her though. After reading about the new learning frameworks in this Lesson, I put them to the test. I learnt *Theme & 12 Deviations* by Sonny Chua, or what I like to call "Chopsticks on Steroids." You can see me in action on our YouTube channel - search for *What You Will Learn* or go to: www.youtube.com/watch?v=eabnjfEaaAI

better way to learn would be to break it down into the little sub-skills. Breaking down a big skill into chunks means you can pick small areas at a time to work on. The obvious ones are the start and end of every hole: driving off the tee and putting. Then you've got all the bits in between - club selection, hitting with a wood VS an iron VS a wedge, hitting from the fairway, hitting from the rough, getting out of a sand bunker, pitching, chipping, bump-and-runs. Rather than stepping straight out onto the golf course, it'd probably be wise to do five sessions of mini golf with a group of mates, then five sessions at the driving range where you get to hit 100 balls without fear of killing someone. By learning each of these individual components one by one, you will eventually learn to "play golf."

Step 1 of this DSSS learning model is Deconstruction.
Remember to ask: "What are the minimal learnable units, the Lego Blocks, I should be starting with?"

Selection

I (Jonesy) once studied in Turkey, and being a (self-perceived) man of culture, tried to pick up the language. In the first lesson, I was given 100 words to learn for the week. While some words were mildly useful, most were not. I found myself exerting a significant cognitive load on words like

LESSON 3 | *Learning*

"horseshoe." This is *not* effective learning... when the hell am I going to need to say horseshoe in Turkish?!

When learning *effectively*, we're saving our brains for the items that will give the best bang for buck. In the previous step, we deconstructed the skill into its smaller components. Now that we've got a whole bunch of Lego Blocks, it's time to choose which blocks we're going to focus on.

Let's be smart about this: we're not going to try to learn *as much as possible*; we're going to try to learn *as little as necessary*. For now, we just want to know enough to get us to competency - we don't need to be world-class just yet. Zooming in on a small selection is going to get us to a reasonable level of skill quite quickly, and then we can focus on perfecting the nitty gritty after that.

Selecting the best bits comes down to the *Pareto Principle* or the *80/20 Rule*. The story goes that Vilfredo Pareto was way ahead of that Occupy Wall Street crew - Pareto discovered an unequal income distribution where 80% of the wealth was held by 20% of the population. Then, while gardening, he found that 80% of the peas he harvested came from the best 20% of pea pods. This 80/20 split seemed to pop up everywhere.

When it comes to learning, we'll also find that 80% of the big skill comes from 20% of the little blocks. On the piano, if we just focus on chords and melody, we'll be able to impress our friends and basically play any modern song we like.

LESSON 3 | *Learning*

On the golf course, if we can drive, chip and putt, we won't embarrass ourselves (too much).

If you want to learn a language, you can do the 80/20 on the 80/20 of the 80/20. There are around 250,000 words in the English dictionary, but the top 25 words (0.01%) unlock 33% of all printed material[16]. The English language would really get old mate Pareto going! The top 100 most commonly used words give us over 50% of published material, and the top 300 words get us to 65%. To be extremely fluent and comfortable in speaking English, we don't need to know all 250,000 words - somewhere around 1,000 to 1,200 will do the trick (if we've selected the best words to learn).

What we learn matters much more than *how* we learn. Picking the right things to focus on is more important than anything else we do in our learning journey. If the highest yield material is selected, we can stuff everything up along the way and *still* be a stunning success (and, of course, choose the *wrong* material, and we may be screwed no matter what).

Step 2 of DSSS is Selection.
Ask: "Which 20% of the blocks should I focus on for 80% (or more) of the outcome I want?"

---

[16] If you're curious, the top 25 most common words used in English are: the, be, to, of, and, a, in, that, have, I, it, for, not, on, with, as, you, do, at, this, but, by, from, they, or. If a foreigner learns those 25 words, they've just learned a third of the words used in the English language.

LESSON 3 | *Learning*

Sequencing

We've deconstructed the skill into its smaller building blocks, and we've selected the most important and highest leverage ones to start with. Now, we need to put these blocks together in the right order.

Although we may end up in the bunker a lot as beginner golfers, learning to hit out of the bunker before we learn to hit from the fairway is a bit like putting the cart before the horse. Or, as Mike Myers would say in *A View From The Top*, putting the emPHASis on the wrong sylLABle.

In his book, *The Art of Learning*, famous chess player Josh Waitzkin talks about how he learned chess rather differently from most people. Generally, we would begin with the start of a game - a full board, all 32 pieces in place. We need to learn what a queen, king, bishop, knight, rook and pawn can/can't do, what directions they can move, and how far. We learn how to kill other pieces, which pieces are more or less important than others, and how to win. That's a hell of a lot to take in!

Instead, Josh's teacher started at the *end*. He had just his king, and he gave Josh a king and one pawn. Now he only needed to know two pieces, not six, and in terms of moves, they were the two most basic (one square at a time). Once Josh could regularly beat his teacher with just a pawn, additional pieces were introduced one by one. By learning these sequentially, he wasn't overwhelmed by the complexity of strategy and tactics - he could focus on one small micro-skill and gradually stack learning blocks from there.

Step 3 of DSSS is Sequencing.
Ask: "In what order should I learn the blocks?"

Stakes

This brings us to the final step: Stakes. When we want to learn something new, we typically set out with the right intention. We plan on sticking to it, pushing through the initial pain and awkwardness until we reach some level of competency. But those early stages of learning are filled with landmines ready to send us flying right back to our comfort zones.

One thing we can do to keep us going on this learning journey is to have some form of consequences built in. As soon as we hit any hurdles or get stuck in a progress plateau, we're probably going to want to throw in the towel... so we need to link real-world consequences to giving up so that we stay on track.

I (Jonesy) implemented some stakes in my attempt at losing weight. Having read one of Ferriss's other books, *The Four Hour Body*[17], I was determined to stick to the Slow Carb Diet for six weeks. I took some unflattering topless 'before' photos of myself and sent them to a trusted group of mates.

---

[17] Part I, Lesson 4, Chapter 14 of the original *The Sh*t They Never Taught You.*

LESSON 3 | *Learning*

I told them that if they caught me NOT following the slow carb diet, and if I hadn't lost 9kg by the time the 6 weeks was up, they were instructed to post these photos publicly. Having these unflattering photos on the line was a good incentive to make me stick to the diet. In the end, I published these 'before and after' photos on our *What You Will Learn* Instagram page anyway, but the potential consequences kept me honest[18].

Aside from these reputational-type consequences, like publicly sharing unflattering photos, other things that could be used as stakes could be monetary in nature. For example, a group of mates chuck in $100 each, and the person who learns the coolest song on the piano by the end of the month wins the cash[19]. Or, you write a cheque to your least favourite organisation (think the opposing political party or your in-laws) and have someone send in the cheque if you give up on learning this new skill too soon.

Step 4 of DSSS is Stakes.
Ask: "How do I set up stakes to create real consequences and guarantee I follow the program?"

---

[18] The 'after' photo in hindsight, wasn't too much better than the 'before' photo. I put the weight back on and regretted the whole escapade. Now there are two unflattering photos on the internet. Anyway, Stakes...

[19] Just like 'The Contest' in *Seinfeld*, where whoever could remain "the master of their domain" the longest took home the kitty.

LESSON 3 | *Learning*

CHAPTER 8
Get Off The Couch

"Put yourself in potentially embarrassing situations on a regular basis just to maintain practice. If you get embarrassed as planned, watch how one year later you are still alive."

Inspired by: **Loserthink,** *by Scott Adams*

I (Jonesy) have a mate who is a bit of a stoner. If he's spending an evening on the grass, he struggles to motivate himself to get off the couch. He calls it "couch lock" - he feels like he's actually stuck to the couch, like he's literally locked into the cushions. Obviously, his body is physically *able* to get up, and presumably, he may even *want* to get up to go do something; he just lacks the specific motivation to get moving.

This feeling of couch lock isn't limited to just pot smokers. We've *all* experienced this before: we want to get up and do something useful or productive but find our brain trapped

LESSON 3 | *Learning*

inside our lazy body and unable to talk it into making that first move. It happens whenever we're tired, unmotivated, anxious, depressed, shy, or just plain lazy. We lie there like a sack of potatoes, powerless to provoke ourselves into action.

Whenever we try to learn something new, we're going to trigger feelings of nervousness and anxiety. Learning to bake, play tennis, or speak in public feels like a mammoth task. We're going to suck at first, probably for a while... so it's a lot easier to stay on the couch and *not* put ourselves through the misery and struggle. We'll get stuck on the couch, so we need to find a way to get up and get moving and start making those first micro-steps towards actual progress.

The secret to overcoming couch lock is to stop thinking of how ambitious and scary, and daunting this objective might be, and start imagining the smallest steps we can take with minimal effort. If you can't talk yourself into practising that new Rachmaninoff piece or writing your best man speech... then just talk yourself into doing something small - start with one scale or one sentence. If you feel you can't even talk yourself into standing up and getting your body moving, talk yourself into moving your pinky finger.

Then move it. Start to wiggle that little pinky. That's all you need to do for now. *Just move your pinky finger.*

LESSON 3 | *Learning*

As you move your pinky, you instantly regain a sense of agency over your body. It's so easy that no matter how locked to the couch you are, no matter how lazy or tired or stressed you are, you can surely manage that little wiggle. From there, you build momentum. Having proved to yourself that you can move your pinky, start moving your ring finger, then your rude finger, and you may as well bring the index finger and the thumb along for the ride too. Next, start to move your hand and your wrist, then your elbow joint, and then your whole arm. Soon enough, you'll be jiggling your whole body and be ready to spring up from the couch and get working on the thing you know you *should* have been doing all along.

Sometimes writing this book felt like a monstrous task, so much so that it crippled us into procrastination. We knew we should've been working on this book, but it was much easier to chill on the couch instead. To cure our couch lock, we talked ourselves (tricked ourselves) into making the smallest possible progress - just writing one sentence. Then, once we had the laptop open and we'd started moving, we often accidentally just kept going and would write a whole page, sometimes even a whole chapter.

The total amount of effort required to put this book together is pretty enormous. But if we zoom in on any particular individual day, the amount of effort required is very manageable (sometimes even negligible). That's how life works: we take continuous microsteps that equate to significant things over time.

Regardless of what it is we want to learn, imagining the entire task ahead isn't going to be helpful; it's actually more likely to overwhelm us into inaction. Instead, combine the DSSS method (Deconstruction, Selection, Sequencing, Stakes) with this cure for couch lock: break down the new skill into its tiny component parts, and just talk yourself into getting off the couch and getting started on the smallest possible thing you can do *right now* with almost no effort. Then build your skills from there, one tiny Lego Block and pinky wiggle at a time.

Stepping Outside Your Lane

Here's some advice you should give your worst enemy: *"Stay in your lane."* We see this trope bandied about online a lot these days, trying to put people back in their place. But of course, if everyone followed this advice, the world as we know it wouldn't exist. Civilization was built entirely by people who dared to venture *outside* of their lane and try something new.

Think of Leonardo da Vinci. He was a pretty talented painter, so he'd be forgiven for staying in his painting lane. If we saw Leonardo at the hospital asking the staff if he

LESSON 3 | *Learning*

could have a dead body so he could dissect and learn about how things work beneath the surface, we'd probably think he'd gone crazy[20]. If he wasn't dragged straight to the insane asylum, at the very least we'd recommend that he should stay in his lane and focus on his artwork. But by daring to venture outside his comfort zone and learn something new, Leonardo opened up all sorts of new doorways. He effectively created the first accurate textbook of human anatomy, but it went unpublished (and took another few centuries for people to rediscover things Leonardo had already documented but never saw the light of day). By broadening his domain to anatomy and biology, he also improved his original lane of painting. By garnering a better understanding of how muscles, tendons and joints worked below the surface; he was able to create the most famous smile of all time: the one belonging to *The Mona Lisa*.

If you're already world-class at something, if you're already at the top of your field in something hyper-specialised, then maybe you should stay in that lane. But for everyone else, a far better strategy is to *leave* our lane as often as possible. The only way to widen our lane is to push our boundaries

---

[20] He actually did this. Apparently, he "acquired" more than 20 dead bodies and cut them open to see how they worked as a way of creating better, more informed, more realistic art. Check out our episode on the *What You Will Learn* podcast for more wild and whacky stories about the great man, *Episode 386: Leonardo da Vinci*

constantly. If we don't try anything new, we're not building our skill stack - and we will never change in a way that will move us toward our vision. If you do what you've always done, you'll get what you've always got.

Sticking to what you know ensures that you stay exactly where you are: stuck on the couch. Learning to take sensible chances outside your lane is one of the best life skills you will ever acquire.

Managing Embarrassment

Learning new things means you're going to make mistakes. No one does things exactly right on the first go, so you're guaranteed to stuff it up. To many people, the simple thought of stuffing things up stops them from ever trying. But as a bunch of great philosophers[21] once said: *"If you never try, you'll never know."* Learning means trying new shit, which means stuffing up. It's par for the course. So get comfortable with being uncomfortable.

The best way to get over embarrassment at stuffing up is to practise it. Practise being embarrassed, and we'll eventually stop being embarrassed. If we regularly put ourselves in potentially embarrassing situations, situations we know we're going to stuff up but learn something from, we'll be far better off.

---

[21] Coldplay in their song *Fix You*.

LESSON 3 | *Learning*

Think about this: the last time you saw someone else do something embarrassing, how long did you think about it? Did you peg them with that one moment for the rest of the time you knew them, or did you have a little chuckle and then forget about it pretty much immediately? I'm tipping it was the latter. When we're the observer, we don't think much of people stuffing little things up, so it's important to realise that other people viewing our embarrassing stuff ups don't care much either.

If you don't know exactly how to do something, you've got a few options. First, you can try to do some quick research, a little bit of googling, and see if you can work it out. Second, you could do nothing. If Plan A doesn't dig up anything substantial, and Plan B leaves you stuck on the couch, your only other option is Plan C: try doing it *wrong*. As long as it's not dangerous, as long as it's not physically or financially disastrous, it's far better to try to do something the wrong way than not at all. Waiting until you know how to do something exactly right is a poor strategy - you could be waiting forever! It's far better to jump in, make mistakes, and see what kind of progress you can make.

Will it be a little embarrassing at first? Yes.

Will you figure it out as you go? Also yes.

LESSON 3 | *Learning*

It's time to get off the couch and give it a crack. It's time to learn.

CHAPTER 9
Deep Practice

"Don't look for the big, quick improvement. Seek the small improvement one day at a time."

Inspired by: **The Talent Code,** *by Dan Coyle*

In this lesson so far, we've been talking about getting off the couch and stepping outside of our lane to try something new. By deconstructing a skill into tiny component parts, you'll be able to quickly learn in a way that takes you from novice to moderately competent in a few short weeks. Now we're going to build on that and start heading toward world-class performance in your new skill. It's time to take those early building blocks you've managed to stack together and accelerate toward a Lego masterpiece.

In essence, we want you to tap into the HSE. This is a highly scientific, rigorously tested, very serious discovery... *The Holy Shit Effect.* The HSE is a mix of admiration and envy when 'talent' seems to suddenly appear out of nowhere.

LESSON 3 | *Learning*

We feel the Holy Shit Effect when we hear Pavarotti hitting that high note in *Nessun Dorma*, or when we see Serena Williams smack a winner down the line, or when we watch a video of Tiger Woods hitting out of a bunker, curling it around a tree, landing on the green, then spinning more than 90 degrees toward the hole[22].

The HSE comes not just from these internationally recognised superstars but also from seeing people we thought were 'just like us'... only now we must accept that they're something different altogether. It's the tingle of surprise we get when the goofy kid from down the street we thought was a no-hoper, is all of a sudden the lead guitarist in a successful rock band. Or when you're helping your daughter with her maths homework, and she's really struggling, but a few short weeks later, she's suddenly teaching you. The Holy Shit Effect is the feeling of: *"Where did THAT come from?!"*

The interesting thing about the HSE is that it only operates in one direction. The observer is flabbergasted - when you see that weird neighbour suddenly shredding an impressive guitar solo, you're bewildered. The owner of that talent, though, isn't surprised; they're even a bit 'meh' about it. This is not false modesty on their behalf. It's standard practice for talent acquisition. They've practised so hard, they've gone

---

[22] If you've got an interest in golf, watch this wild shot and try not to say "holy shit" after you see it: https://www.youtube.com/watch?v=Rl_oUUQlk24, or search on YouTube for 'That unbelievable Tiger Woods fairway bunker shot' from WGC Mexico 2019.

through the struggles it took to develop the talent, and they know how much hard work went into building that skill. It is now somewhat 'normal' and unsurprising to them.

Take a gymnast, for example. When a gymnast does a double backflip off an apparatus, they don't think: *"Okay, I'm going to push off with my legs, 30% power from the front foot and 70% power from the back foot a quarter of a second later, arch my back, tuck my chin to my chest, bring my hips around..."* No. They just think: *"Do a double backflip."* This move has been honed through years and years of Deep Practice and it has become just a normal part of their routine. The brain tells the body what to do, and the body knows from all the practice, so the body can take over and do the rest of the job.

What separates us from the elite performers is not some impassable chasm. It's purely the cumulation of weeks and months and years of Deep Practice, building skill from the ground up like scaffolding - beam by beam, bolt by bolt, link by link, level by level.

If you want to learn a skill that makes people say: *"Holy Shit!"* then you'll need to follow the three rules of Deep Practice.

LESSON 3 | *Learning*

Rule 1: *Chunk It Up*

The art of Deep Practice is kind of like the way a nature documentary maker approaches a scene: they begin with a wide angle to see the whole jungle, then they zoom in to see a bug crawling on a leaf, then watch as it gets slurped up by a lizard's tongue in slow motion.

Step One: Absorb The Whole Thing

The Spartak Tennis Club in Moscow had only one indoor court, yet they cranked out a volcanic eruption of tennis talent. At one point, this one tiny tennis club had more Top 20 ranked tennis players than the entire United States combined. Famous names like Anna Kournikova, Marat Safin, Dinara Safina, Mikhail Youzhny and Elena Dementieva are all products of Spartak.

This one tennis court produced multiple world number ones and multiple grand slam titles using a rather unconventional teaching style. From the age of five all the way through to the pros on the international circuit, all players are put through a practice routine called *imitatsiya*. This drill uses imaginary balls - the players walk slowly around the court practising different shots in slow motion. If you watch this in action, it looks more like a ballet class than a tennis lesson. The players are absorbing the whole game of tennis without yet focusing on any specific micro-skills - they're effectively building the scaffolding frame and laying the foundations before going into the finer details. They're preparing the canvas upon which they're about to paint their masterpiece.

This is the first step of the first rule of Deep Practice - absorbing the whole thing in its entirety. If we want to learn tennis, we must get an understanding of the flow of the game before working on any specific shots. If we want to learn Ronaldhino's famous *elastico* soccer move, we would watch a bunch of YouTube videos of him executing it to perfection before having a crack. If we want to cook a new dish, we might watch a video of Gordon Ramsay or Donna Hay cooking it first before opening up the pantry and mixing stuff together. If we want to learn a new Mozart piece on the piano, we'd open up Spotify and listen to it a couple of times, so we have a mental recording of how it's *supposed* to sound before opening the sheet music or striking the first key.

Like that documentary maker, you're viewing the whole landscape. Once your subconscious knows what you want your body to do, it will start to imitate it, and you'll be well on your way to HSE'ing this new skill before you've even started.

Step Two: Break It Into Chunks

The musical equivalent of the Spartak Tennis Club in Russia is the Meadowmount School of Music in upstate New York. Their alumni include violinist Joshua Bell and cellist Yo-Yo

LESSON 3 | *Learning*

Ma. Students at Meadowmount are able to learn new pieces in hyperdrive - the process they teach enables you to learn about 500% faster than you normally would.

Normally, if you wanted to learn a new piece, you'd grab the sheet music and start playing from the first note of the first bar of the first line and work your way through to the end. Seems pretty logical. But not at Meadowmount. At Meadowmount, they take the sheet of music, chop it up into long horizontal strips, chuck them all in a bag, shake them up, and pick out a random line of the music. They play around with the rhythm, playing things slightly syncopated[23]. Playing it in these weird ways makes the brain (and fingers) work a bit harder, which counterintuitively makes the notes stick quicker.

Once they've mastered one line, it's back to the bag to grab another random chunk. When the bag is empty and they've mastered each individual line, they get the 'normal' sheet music, playing it in the proper order, and it's just a matter of stitching together all the bits they already know how to play.

This chunking method turns out to be far quicker than trying to learn the song from start to finish. By zooming in on just small sections at a time and mastering them, you're training your brain, your fingers and your ear gradually, line by line, rather than trying to do the whole thing at once.

---

[23] Instead of playing it straight like a dog would walk (consistent and even, dah-dah-dah-dah) they play it more like a horse gallop (dah-dum dah-dum).

Step Three: Slow It Down

The third step of the first rule of chunking might sound a little strange: practice really *really* slowly. Like, slow it down to what you think is ridiculously slow, then go even slower. Practise at a glacial pace.

As Abraham Lincoln once said: *"I am slow to learn, but also slow to forget what I have learned. My mind is like a piece of steel - very hard to scratch anything on it, but once it's on it, almost impossible to rub it out."* Going slow allows us to attend more closely to errors, creating a higher degree of precision with each firing. We'll avoid those little errors at the start, meaning we'll never program in the *wrong* stuff (which is almost impossible to eradicate once it's in the brain).

Going back to 2008, when I (Ashto) was preparing for my Grade 8 piano exam, I was playing Handel's *Air and Variations*. Almost 15 years later, having played this piece at exams and concerts, it popped up on my Spotify while I was writing this book. I was baffled to hear one note right at the end, in this little fill section before the big finish, that didn't sound quite right to me. I thought maybe the world-class professional on the recording must've fudged it (surely they were wrong, not me...). I went to check the sheet music and couldn't believe my eyes! I'd been playing a B this whole time, but the music said it should've been an A. My brain knows it should be an A now, but years of practice has that B so deeply ingrained I don't think I'll ever be able to change it...

That's why going slow is so important at the start. We're coding the body. Those first few times we practise, we're telling the body exactly what to do. Our body learns, and our body remembers. If we code in a little bug, it's probably going to stay there forever. So, by going ridiculously slow at the start, you'll be able to practise your new skill with complete precision. Once you know exactly what you're doing and you're executing it perfectly every time, you can gradually speed it up to a normal pace.

This is easy to do for things like music, where you can slow down the speed at which you play, but it's equally applicable to other physical skills too. Like those tennis players playing imaginary tennis super slowly. By going super slowly, you'll train your body and brain to do it perfectly from the start.

Rule 2: *Repeat It*

There is no substitute for repetition. Let us repeat that: there is no substitute for repetition. No amount of thinking, talking, reading, watching, imagining or visualising can replace actually *doing*. Nothing we can do is more effective in building the skill than executing the action and fixing any errors.

Think of it this way - what's the easiest way to make LeBron James start missing jump shots or for Chee-Yun to start fudging notes on the violin? Don't let them practise for a year. Vladimir Horowitz, the virtuoso pianist who kept performing into his 80s, said: *"If I skip practice for a day, I notice... If I skip practice for two days, my wife notices... If I skip practice for three days, the world notices."*

This applies to all skills. Say you were School Captain in high school, and you gave speeches at assembly every week. Then for a few years of uni, you have limited public speaking opportunities. When you start your first job and need to stand up in the team meeting to give your monthly report, your skill of 'public speaking' will be out of practice, and you'll be far more nervous and stumbly than you used to be.

Just to repeat it one more time: there is no substitute for repetition.

Rule 3: *Learn To* Feel *It*

World-renowned string teacher Skye Carman taught a class to young up-and-coming musicians called *"How To Practice."* As the former concertmaster of the Holland Symphony, she asked the young kids in her class: *"How many of you practise more than five hours a day?"* Four nerds shot their hands up. *"Good for you,"* she said, *"I could never have done that when I was a kid."*

LESSON 3 | *Learning*

But then she asked the more important question: *"What do you DO when you practise? What's the first thing you do at the beginning of those five hours?"* There was a bit of awkward silence. Eventually, one kid spoke: *"I dunno... I guess I tune-up, then I play some Bach or something."*

Skye let out a long and judgemental sigh. She said: *"I bet you all just PLAY, don't you... you pick a piece you like, then begin fooling around."* They all nodded. *"Well, that's CRAZY! Do you think athletes do that? Pull on their footy boots, then go out and play a game?! NO! They warm up. They prepare their muscles, the key ingredients they need to succeed. They start with some simple skills, kicking a ball just a short distance. They're getting some FEEL. For musicians, your key ingredient is your EAR - you need to warm up your ear and get some feel for it. FIRST, you tune your instrument, THEN you tune your ear. Only then can you start to play."*

These poor little kids would've had no idea what hit them or who this crazy lady was that had walked into their classroom. But she had a point. Once you've attained the skill on an intellectual level, once you know exactly what you need to do and when and how you need to do it, you need to drill it in so deeply that you can just *feel* it. It should become subconscious.

If you're a violinist and a string is out of tune, it should *bother* you on a deep, visceral level. It should be uncomfortable

LESSON 3 | *Learning*

to hear a note that isn't quite right. Crazy old Skye showed her kids an example. She asked them to close their eyes, and she played a long consistent G string. The kids were all sitting there with their eyes closed, enjoying the pleasant sound. Then, as she kept playing that note, she grabbed the tuning peg and twisted it ever so slightly. You could see all the kids' faces scrunch up, almost as if they were in pain.

This is the level you need to get to, this intuition about when things are right, and when they're off.

Getting to this level of skill is when that one-way Holy Shit Effect kicks in - when the observer sees some incredible performance, but the talent owner doesn't understand what all the fuss is about. I (Ashto) once played in a band with a few mates, and it was a hell of a lot of fun. We spent all summer practising for our debut gig, and it stands out in the memory as probably my favourite summer so far. But when TomKat would rip out this nice guitar solo, then say *"Asho, your turn!"* I had absolutely no freaking idea what to do... I could play classical pieces and follow sheet music (except for that one wrong note I'd stuffed up for ten years), but when I had to go off script, I was paralysed.

My Dad has played guitar in bands his whole life, and he can seriously shred. One day, we had a jam together, Dad on guitar and me on piano, then after a couple of verses, Dad laid down an absolute face-melter of a solo. So I asked him: *"Dad, how do you do solos?"* He said: *"I don't know, I guess you just kinda... go for it."* This was a classic example of the Holy Shit Effect - to me it was so good I couldn't even comprehend ever getting to that level. To him it was nothing special; he just 'went for it.' He'd got to the 'unconscious competency' level of performance where he didn't even know what he was doing; he just felt it.

I had to work it out on my own. I did a bunch of research into the theory behind it - the chord progressions, the pentatonic scale, and what notes you should/shouldn't play. I looked at jazz solos VS rock solos VS pop solos. I stumbled around a lot on the keys, trying different combinations and sequences of notes, learning what sounded good and what didn't. I sucked at first (obviously), but the more I practised, the more I improved.

Now, I can whip out a solo in just about any song I play. When I'm fooling around at home, I'll play a few verses normally, and then I'll freestyle and let loose.

The funny thing is, if anyone came to me and asked how to improvise a solo, I wouldn't have a clue how to explain it. I just feel it. The only thing I could muster would be: *"I don't know, I guess you just kinda... go for it."*

LESSON 3 | *Learning*

Baby Steps

Of all the images that communicate the sensation of Deep Practice, perhaps the best is babies learning to walk. At first, they're staggering around, barely able to stand in one spot... then eventually, something clicks, and they get to the point where they can walk.

A study by American and Norwegian researchers looked at what helped babies improve at walking. They discovered that the 'obvious' factors had nothing to do with it. The height, weight, centre of gravity, age, brain development, or any other innate trait had nothing to do with walking skills. Instead, the only thing that mattered was the *amount of time* they practised. The more they tried it out, the more they stumbled around, and the quicker they got the hang of it.

Deep Practice feels like a baby trying to walk. At first, there's a lot of staggering and fumbling, a lot of jolts and stop-starts. We're desperately trying to get towards our goal, but it's clumsy, it's wobbly, it's an uncomfortable feeling that any sensible person would try to avoid...

The staggering babies embody the deepest truth about Deep Practice: in order to get good, it's helpful to be willing, or even enthusiastic, about being bad. Baby steps are the royal road to skill.

LESSON 3 | *Learning*

After understanding the "Three Rules of Deep Practice," I (Ashto) saw a way to learn new things more effectively than ever before. I wanted to expand my repertoire of piano pieces, so I bought a book called *The Library of Piano Classics* and started working my way through them. But I didn't do it my 'old' way of just starting at the beginning; I engaged the Deep Practice way. Chunking it up (absorbing the whole thing by listening to recordings on Spotify, breaking it into chunks by tackling random lines at a time, playing around with the rhythm and timing to make it harder but stickier in the brain, slowing it right down). Repeating it. Learning to feel it.

The first song I learned was Beethoven's *Moonlight Sonata*, one of my grandmother's favourites. It is an intermediate piece, obviously brand new to me, but well within my level of ability. On the first day, I was stumbling around and making mistakes, and going over the same little things again and again. Every time I made a mistake, I instantly went back and tried to fix it, so I wasn't coding in the wrong stuff. Often, I'd play the same wrong chord three or four

LESSON 3 | *Learning*

times, getting slightly more frustrated and aggressive each time but pushing through the struggle.

Then my wife Alison said something that felt like a slap in the face: "You sound like a drunk elephant... What happened? You used to be so good?!" Previously, a comment like that would have sent me running to my room crying. If I had a Fixed Mindset[24], it would've shattered my self-image. I would only play old songs I already knew, over and over, in an attempt to show how 'good' I was. But thankfully, I'd read this book, and that slap in the face was actually the best compliment she could've given me. Playing things wrong, immediately correcting the errors, repeating the same thing over and over... to an outside observer, it may have sounded like a drunk elephant, but to me, it sounded like learning.

Using this learning framework, *Moonlight Sonata* was the quickest piece I'd ever learnt. A day and a half later, when I played Alison the whole song perfectly from start to finish, with all the right

---

[24] If you're unfamiliar with this term, it's one of the most important concepts we've ever read. Check out Lesson 2 of *The Sh* They Never Taught You*.

LESSON 3 | *Learning*

pedalling and dynamics and accents and transitions, all she could say was: "Holy Shit... where did THAT come from?!"

Lesson 4

fear.

LESSON 4 | *Fear*

Fear is inevitable. We're all afraid of something. Afraid to change, afraid to stay the same. Afraid to speak out, afraid to stay quiet. Afraid to overcook the steak, afraid to undercook the chicken.

Fear is understandable. If we're not certain what the outcome may be, we're allowed to be a little afraid of what may be around the corner.

But even though fear is inevitable, and fear is understandable, we can't let fear stand in our way. We can't let fear stop us. We can't let fear hold us back from working toward our vision, or changing ourselves, or trying new things.

Fear can be overcome. Perhaps it is not what you *think* it is. Perhaps the reason you think you're afraid isn't the real reason at all. By reframing your fears, you'll be far more likely to overcome them and keep learning and changing on your way to achieving your vision.

CHAPTER 10
Fear Reframe #1: *WHY Do You Fear?*

"We are not determined by our experiences, but the meaning we give them is self-determining."

Inspired by: **The Courage To Be Disliked,**
by Ichiro Kishimi and Fumitake Koga

Old Model: *Freud's Aetiology*

Sigmund Freud is one of the most influential psychologists of all time. He had a few strange ideas, such as the Oedipus complex - old Freudy reckons all young boys go through a phase where they want to murder their fathers and have sex with their mothers[25]. However, he also made some serious headway in the field of neurology, such as founding psychoanalysis - a clinical method for treating issues and concerns through dialogue between a therapist and a patient.

---

[25] Perhaps that whole theory is some kind of Freudian slip...

LESSON 4 | *Fear*

Freud brought us the theories of the ego, the superego and the id and highlighted things like depression and defence mechanisms, as well as identifying many broader mental illnesses or disorders.

As part of this work, he leaned heavily on the idea that the past dictates our present and future. Things that have happened in our past play an important role in how we behave in the present and the outcomes we'll get in the future. Take his theory on "defence mechanisms," for instance. Freud said that we did (or didn't do) certain things unconsciously to protect ourselves from anxiety-producing thoughts and feelings. Bad things happened to us in our past, so we (subconsciously) came up with these defence mechanisms to protect our psyche against it happening to us again. Some defence mechanisms include denial (pretending something isn't happening, so we don't have to face the associated emotions), projection (misattributing our views as someone else's, pretending other people are thinking and feeling the things that we are actually feeling deep down inside but are too afraid to admit[26]), and compartmentalisation (separating our life into different independent segments in order to protect most elements of it).

Let's take "fear" as an example, specifically a fear of public speaking. Public speaking is something almost everyone is afraid of - it ranks as the #1 most common fear in many

---

[26] This is probably what was happening with his whole Oedipus thing.

studies. According to Freud's theory, a fear of public speaking would have been created as a result of something that had happened in the past. Perhaps when you were in first grade at school, your teacher asked you to read a page of a book aloud, and you butchered it so badly that all the kids laughed at you. The shame and embarrassment you felt because of this was something you vowed you never wanted to feel again. So, your Freudian brain got to work, cooking up a plan to help you avoid those negative feelings in the future. Your brain created a 'fear of public speaking' - that way, the next time an opportunity to speak in public arose, you could shyly decline or find an excuse to get out of it. You may not even remember that day in first grade; you can't recall that specific scenario ever happening; you just know that now, as an adult, you're afraid of speaking in front of a large group.

This model of "cause-and-effect" is the common understanding of how our defence mechanisms, like fear, work. Something bad happened in the past, something we don't want to happen again, so our brain creates a fear to help us avoid putting ourselves through the same misery in the future.

This concept or way of viewing the world is known as *aetiology*. Aetiology is all about studying causation, finding reasons for current behaviour based on the past, and uncovering the cause-and-effect patterns that drive us. It says that if bad shit happened in our past, we will be a little messed up from it.

It kind of makes sense - if something terrible happened to you when you were young, your brain would morph in ways that tried to prevent similar things from happening in the future. If you ask a girl out on a date and she rejects you, your brain will concoct some kind of fear of talking to girls to help you avoid future rejections (from personal experience, we can both attest to that one).

Past negative experiences create these psychological reactions. It's understandable why you haven't put yourself out there to learn new things, to make a change, to pursue your vision - you've had some bad shit happen in the past, so parts of your brain are holding you back from fully committing to a new attitude. With everything you've faced before now, it's no wonder you haven't accomplished everything you'd hoped for.

What About Oprah?

But hang on, if experiences from our past create psychological blocks that hold us back from doing certain things in the present that therefore prevent us from achieving our fullest potential... how do some people become successful? How do some people build successful businesses, get promoted to the C-suite, become world-class athletes, achieve international

LESSON 4 | *Fear*

fame? Perhaps their upbringing was all roses, and nothing bad ever happened to them. That would fit with the Freud cause-and-effect model - there were no negative causes, so there were no negative effects.

What about Oprah?

Oprah Winfrey is, without doubt one of the most recognisable people in the world. We didn't even have to say "Winfrey" since you already knew who we were talking about just from the word "Oprah." For 25 years, *The Oprah Winfrey Show* was broadcast nationally and internationally, averaging 40 million weekly viewers. She was dubbed "The Queen of All Media," became a self-made billionaire, was ranked among the most influential people in the world, and is one of the greatest philanthropists in history.

If applying the cause-and-effect theory, one would assume with all this greatness that Oprah had a flawless upbringing. But if you know anything about Oprah's story... you'll know that this isn't the case. Oprah did, in fact, face plenty of adversity when she was younger. Oprah's parents weren't together when she was born - they were 18 and 20 at the time, so Oprah was raised by a teenage single mother. Her mum soon left to find stable work, so Oprah was sent to live with her grandmother. Oprah reports that her grandmother was tough and strict, and Oprah would cop beatings and abuse for the slightest missteps. They say: "Don't cry over spilt milk," but if

LESSON 4 | Fear

Oprah accidentally spilled any milk, she was whooped for it. Any inability to keep quiet or stay still resulted in a whack or two, and then she was told not to cry, to suck it up and put on a smile for her grandmother or face another whack.

Her grandmother fell ill when Oprah was six, so she was sent back to live with her mother. Her mother lived in a boarding house, and the owner wouldn't let a child stay in the room, so she was forced to sleep on the porch.

At the age of nine, Oprah was raped by her 19-year-old cousin. As the years went on, she was vulnerable and continually abused. She was sexually assaulted by a family friend and then by an uncle. The aftermath of these traumas meant Oprah no longer valued herself. She didn't understand that she could set boundaries over her own body, and she became quite promiscuous. Without an understanding of the consequences of being sexually active, she fell pregnant at age 14.

Her mother didn't know what to do with her, so she sent Oprah to live with her father. She was so afraid to tell her father what happened that she hid it as long as she could... until a swollen belly quickly gave it away. The day she confessed to her father that she was pregnant was also the day she went into premature labour. A baby boy was born, but he didn't stand a chance. A week later, having never left the hospital and having never been held by his mother, the little boy died.

Now, knowing this, we can't say that bad shit didn't happen to Oprah. Following Freud's line of reasoning, the cause-and-effect nature of psychology would mean that Oprah would never trust another human being again. Her parents abandoned her, her grandmother beat her, her cousin raped her, her uncle abused her, and she lost a child when she was a young teenager. Aetiology would tell us that Oprah would develop a severe fear of intimacy as a defence mechanism. Anyone dealt this set of cards would be forgiven for crawling into their shell and never putting themselves out there again.

Oprah took a different path. Oprah's TV show focused on self-improvement; she communicated with a vulnerable, confessional tone, approached things from an emotional perspective, and connected with others to help them overcome their own adversities.

Clearly, there's something not quite right about Freud's theory.

New Model: *Adler's Teleology*

While Freud was thinking about getting it on with his mum, another Austrian psychologist came onto the scene. Alfred Adler, who went to the University of Vienna about 15 years after Freud did, developed some theories of his own, like the inferiority complex, the importance of birth order, and Gemeinschaftsgefühl (the idea that helping others and contributing to a group is how an individual feels a sense of

LESSON 4 | *Fear*

worth and belonging, whether to their family or community or society more broadly). Adler founded the "school of individual psychology," which is a pretty weak name given it's not really about the individual as much as it is about the environment and the people around them.

While they had a lot of similarities, one key distinction in the approaches between Freud and Adler was the difference in how they viewed fear and emotions. Freud's *aetiology* was all about cause and effect: things that happened in the past created emotions and fears that impacted how we behave in the present. Adler, on the other hand, was all about *teleology*, which purported that we do things not because of our past but because of what we hope to achieve in the future. Teleology tries to explain things not based on what caused it, but rather in terms of the purpose it serves.

Let's look now at the fear of public speaking through a teleological lens. Teleology says that we do (or don't do) things based on what we hope to achieve. As a result, the fear we feel about public speaking must have something to do with the future, not the past. If our goal is to *not* step outside our comfort zone, to stay safe, to avoid risk, to avoid potential embarrassment and shame - then we'll cook up a fear of public speaking in service of those future goals. Rather than saying that we are afraid because the last time we spoke in front of a group, something bad happened (aetiology), we're saying that we're afraid because we want to avoid negative things in the future (teleology). Teleology is concerned with the purpose of a phenomenon, and in this case, the purpose of the fear of public speaking is to avoid future embarrassment.

Fear Is Manufactured

We can look at other examples of this in action. Jonesy has a mate (who we won't name for obvious reasons) who barely goes outside. He doesn't have a job, he plays video games most of the day, and he rarely goes out to see friends. He has no romantic interests, no aspirations, and if we're brutally honest, he isn't really doing *anything* with his life.

Freud's view of this would be that he has social anxiety due to past traumas. Freud would dig into his past to uncover the causes of this behaviour. He'd probably ask if his mum was sexually appealing, really trying to prove that it's not just him who thinks that.

Adler's way of looking at this would be to work out the purpose of this behaviour; he would try to work out what he hopes to get out of doing nothing. Perhaps he doesn't want to risk failure in any form, so if he doesn't ever try, he can't ever fail. Perhaps he likes being coddled - he likes his mum doing his washing and his dad cooking his meals, so by being a bit of a dropkick, he gets to stay in the nest and keep being looked after. In order to stay safe and comfortable in the future, he acts like a no-hoper in the present.

I (Ashto) had some less-than-ideal behaviour of my own. In 2020 I ghost-wrote a book on behalf of a client. It was a fantastic opportunity and a well-paid gig. I went through a company's entire 150+ year history, covering six or seven generations of their family tree. The end result was pretty impressive (if I do say so myself) - the book looked awesome, and most importantly, the clients were super happy.

A few months after I was done, a similar opportunity to write a book for someone presented itself. I had to put together a little pitch as to how I would structure the book. I was really excited about this project, so I put it at the top of my to-do list. But after a week of "thinking," I hadn't made a whole lot of progress. Weeks then turned to months. I'd built it up too much in my brain and couldn't even start.

When I finally knuckled down and did the work, the "pitch" ended up being a simple three-paragraph email with a couple of mockups. That's all it took. The problem was, it was almost a year later! The prospect had lost interest and moved on (understandably... they probably wondered how long it would take me to write a 250-page book if it took me a year to write three paragraphs!).

In hindsight, through Adler's eyes, I can see what happened. I didn't want to get rejected. I didn't want the "thanks, but no thanks" reply email. I didn't want to try and fail - I thought I had an awesome idea, and I didn't want it to get knocked back. Rejection would mean I probably wasn't as good as I thought I was... and I wanted to maintain that flawless self-image. So, in service of the goal of maintaining that self-image in my brain, I avoided future rejection by procrastinating in the present.

Fear Jiu-Jitsu

Think about your own fears. Perhaps, until now, you assumed that your fears and actions were driven by things that had happened to you in the past. There is now a different story you can tell yourself: the things you fear and the actions you take in the present are done in service of a future purpose.

To change the fear, you need to change the way you look at it. Doing a little bit of mental jiu-jitsu can help reframe fear and even make it disappear.

If your future goal is to avoid embarrassment, it will lead to avoiding taking risks now. Steering clear of public speaking helps you attain the goal of not saying the wrong thing in front of a group, so your brain manufactures a fear of public speaking. To kill that fear of public speaking, rather than trying to squash the fear head-on, you can change the future goal - your present actions will then change as a result. If you realise that the future goal is not to avoid embarrassment but actually to learn and grow, your brain will find a way to do it. When your goal is to improve your skills, and you know the only way to improve your skills is to practise, the feeling that you used to call "the fear of public speaking" might still be there, but now the feeling is "the nervous excitement of trying something new and different."

By shifting your vision, teleology says that fear will go away. You'll change your present actions to serve your future goals. You'll be keen to try new things - you know you're going to stuff up, but you'll learn and improve along the way. Public speaking is no longer something to be feared; it's now the only way you can realise your vision.

CHAPTER 11
Fear Reframe #2: *WHAT Do You Fear?*

"Pushing through fear is less frightening than living with the underlying fear that comes from a feeling of helplessness."

Inspired by: **Feel The Fear And Do It Anyway,** *by Susan Jeffers*

Thanks to Adler and teleology, we now have a new way of looking at fears. We have a way to reframe *why* we fear - in service of some future purpose. We have a fear of heights because we don't want to fall and die, so that fear keeps us closer to the ground. We have a fear of enclosed spaces because we don't want to suffocate and die, so that fear keeps us out in the open. We have a fear of public speaking because we don't want to stuff up and die (well, maybe not actually die, but it might feel like it), so that fear makes us keep our head down and play it safe.

LESSON 4 | *Fear*

There is more fear reframing we can do; this time around *what* we fear. Fear is endemic in our society. We fear beginnings, and we fear endings. We fear change, and we fear staying stuck. We fear success, and we fear failure. We fear living, and we fear dying. You may have fears around asserting yourself, making decisions, changing jobs, being alone, getting old, losing a loved one, or a fear of intimacy. There is a seemingly endless list of potential fears. Fears span all aspects of our lives - health, wealth, career, business, relationships... and everything in between. The only common denominator between fears is that they all hold us back in some way. They keep us from trying new things, embracing change, and fulfilling our vision.

Whenever we take a chance, whenever we enter unfamiliar territory, whenever we put ourselves out into the world in some new way in pursuit of a change toward achieving our goals, we experience fear. Very often, this fear keeps us from making progress and moving ahead with our lives. Often, we short-circuit ourselves by choosing the path that is most comfortable: the path we're already on.

But once you know how to reframe *what* you're afraid of, you'll be able to move past some of your usual excuses for staying "safe" (AKA staying *stuck*) and develop techniques for taking control of your life.

Level 1 Fears

When we're trying to work out exactly what it is we're afraid of, we'll find that all fears can be broken down into three levels. The first of these levels is the *surface story*, the things we can name and often use to explain our actions or inactions. "I'm scared of spiders" is one of these surface stories - it does the job of conveying why we don't want to go into a cave, but it's pretty basic.

There are two groups of these Level 1 "surface story" fears:

- The first group are the things that *happen* to us - death, illness, change, accidents, war, natural disasters, loss of financial security, being alone, children leaving home, ageing, retirement, becoming disabled, losing a loved one.
- The second group are those requiring *action*: making decisions, changing careers, re-training or going back to study, giving birth, raising a child, driving, job interviews, public speaking, losing weight, making new friends, ending relationships, beginning relationships.

The insidious quality of fear is that it tends to permeate all areas of our lives. If you've ever feared any of these things, you're certainly not alone. Plus, you can probably add plenty of your own fears to these lists. Ultimately, these Level 1 fears are the obvious fears you'd usually point to and can name.

Level 2 Fears

If we dig a little deeper into each of these Level 1 fears, we'll find a few commonalities lurking beneath. When we drill below the surface we'll find they all are related to some kind of inner state of mind. While the Level 1 fears we rattled off are fears about situations (either things we have to do or things that happen to us), Level 2 fears are fears about the ego.

The list of Level 2 fears is a lot shorter:

- Rejection
- Disapproval
- Success
- Failure
- Loss of Image
- Being Vulnerable
- Helplessness

Let's say, for example, you had a Level 2 fear of rejection. This can manifest itself in a few different Level 1 fears. Fear of rejection could pop up in the career realm as a fear of job interviews. You don't want to get turned down, as this would spark your fear of rejection, so you don't apply for jobs that you might think are above your level of experience. You're only interested in applying for jobs you're sure you can get, which limits you to quite basic jobs, meaning you never really challenge yourself or climb the career ladder. Fear of rejection can also pop up in the personal realm, meaning you don't strive for fulfilling romantic relationships. You keep your guard up, never allowing yourself to share your true feelings in case they aren't reciprocated. This means your relationships will stay at surface level, and you'll never really get to know another person or develop your relationship further. You'll hold yourself back from trying to make new friends as well, meaning your friendship circle will remain quite small, and you won't benefit from a broad, strong personal network.

Rejection is rejection, and it can happen in all areas of your personal and professional life, so this Level 2 fear creeps into a wide range of different areas. As a result of this permeating fear, you begin to protect yourself. You close off. You limit yourself. You begin to shut out the world around you. Of course... people won't feel close to you... and you end up getting rejected! This fear is a bit of a self-fulfilling prophecy - the fear of rejection led you to take actions that ensured you got rejected.

If we do this same exercise with all our vast Level 1 fears, we'll find that they all drill down to a small handful of Level 2 fears. For example, Level 1 fears of illness, ageing, war, having a child, losing weight and ending relationships all boil down to a Level 2 fear of helplessness. If you list out your current fears, you'll probably find they're mostly situation-oriented (Level 1), but if you go a tad further, you'll uncover the Level 2 ego fear that's really driving them.

Level 3 Fears

Level 1 fears are all about external situations. When we dig deeper, we find that Level 2 fears are about inner states of mind. But there is still more we can uncover.

Level 3 fears get down to the real nitty gritty. In fact, Level 3 fears aren't really *fears* (plural); there is just one Level 3 *fear*. It's the biggest one of all, the one that keeps you stuck.

Level 3 Fear is the fear that: *"I can't handle it."*

If we follow the example of the Level 1 fear of job interviews, which is really a Level 2 fear of rejection, it boils down to the Level 3 fear: *"I can't handle it."* If you miss out on getting that job, your brain goes berserk: "I'll never get a job again, nobody wants me, I'll be broke, I'll be homeless, I'll lose everything I've worked for, my career is over." You immediately go to the worst-case scenario, doomsday planning mode. You don't think: "Hey, this was just one job, I'll try again for the next one, and I'll be okay." You think deep down that this isn't a minor setback, it's a major one! And you worry that you might be unable to handle it.

At the bottom of every one of your fears is simply the fear that you can't handle whatever life may bring.

You can see how this translates to all Level 1 and Level 2 fears. I can't handle this illness. I can't handle making a mistake. I can't handle losing money. I can't handle failure. I can't handle rejection.

LESSON 4 | *Fear*

In addition to Adler's reframing of *why* we fear, we now have a way to reframe what we fear.

So What's The Solution?

You're probably not blown away by this revelation. You might be thinking: *"Is that all you've got for me?"* But this is actually some really bloody good news! Since our fears all boil down to the feeling that we can't handle it, the solution is simple: become the type of person that *can* handle it. Learn and change and develop and grow in a way that makes you the type of person that can cope with anything the world throws at you and come out the other side even stronger.

We don't have to try to change anything in the outside world. Fear of war doesn't mean we have to become a president or prime minister so that we can negotiate with other world leaders to avoid hostile conflicts - it just means that you need to build yourself up to be prepared for war if it comes along. Fear of losing money doesn't mean we have to pull all our cash out of investments and stash it under our mattress - it just means we need to develop the skills and attitudes required to bounce back from an economic downturn. Fear of rejection or the fear of flubbing a job interview doesn't mean we have to try and bribe the interviewee with sexual favours or avoid job interviews altogether - it just means we need to realise that if we get rejected from a job interview, we can handle it by applying for another job and trying again.

LESSON 4 | *Fear*

All you have to do in order to diminish your fear is to develop more trust in your ability to handle whatever comes your way. Since there is only one universal fear, the fear that you can't handle it... if you knew you could handle anything that came your way, what would you possibly have left to fear? *Nothing!*

A lack of trust in yourself is the source of all your fears. Those fears keep you from achieving what you want in life and attaining your vision. Knowing this one root cause now enables you to have a laser-like focus on what needs to change: your attitude. You don't need to scatter your efforts in an attempt to address *all* those Level 1 fears individually. You don't need to try to overcome your fear of public speaking, your fear of losing money, your fear of making new friends, and your fear of snakes. You can solve your fears with one significant change: developing more trust in yourself and your ability to handle any situation you're in.

Keep working at it and practising until you get to the point where you can look in the mirror and honestly say to yourself: *Whatever happens, I can handle it!*

LESSON 4 | *Fear*

CHAPTER 12
The Most Significant Struggle

"Your fears are a kind of prison that confines you within a limited range of action. The less you fear, the more power you will have and the more fully you will live."

Inspired by: **The 50th Law,** *by Robert Greene*

There is no shortage of gangsters spitting out phat raps. Even I (Jonesy) made a song in Year 9, gloatingly rapping about how I'd been shot eight times (whilst holding a teddy bear - not sure what I was going for there). Most rappers are full of it. But not Curtis Jackson. His life story is one of someone who confronted and embraced challenges fearlessly, growing into the person we simply know today as 50 Cent.

Up until the year 2000, 50 Cent was a street-hustling nobody. He'd started a compelling career dealing drugs on his corner, but knew he had to make a transition. For him, it meant getting into the music business. After a long time hustling, he finally earned his first record deal. His vision was for his music career to carry him all the way out of Southside Queens. The album was called *The Power of the Dollar.*

It would be an understatement to say things didn't go as planned. In May of that year, another gangster shot nine bullets into 50 while he was hopping out of the car to buy his morning milk. One of the bullets went right through his jaw and nearly killed him. In a flash, the momentum he had built completely reversed. Columbia Records cancelled his album, and no other producer wanted to go near such a dangerous man.

One day his future held prospects of fame and fortune. The next, he hit rock bottom. He thought it would almost have been better to die than stay like that.

But as he lay in bed at his grandma's house, listening to the radio, something occurred to him. All the other gangsters on the radio were pansies. Their lyrics didn't reflect any reality of the streets, most likely because they were performing to what the studio producers requested, as opposed to writing about what was really happening on the ground.

This wasn't a time to sit down and wallow in his pain. These bullets gave him an opportunity. He had never been a fake studio gangster, and now he had nine bullet wounds

LESSON 4 | *Fear*

to prove it. He used this moment to convert his anger into a campaign that would change the foundations of hip-hop.

All his obstacles (no money, no connections, just nine bullet holes and a price on his head) could be turned into opportunities. He literally had nothing to lose.

50 disappeared to a friend's house and got to work each day. Unlike the other wannabees, he had no executives to try and please. He could go as hard as he wanted. In the Summer of 2001, just as people began to forget about him, he released his first song: *Fuck You*. The title was sent directly to the gangsters who shot him, defying his wannabe assassins publicly. They'd have to finish 50 off for good if they wanted to shut him up.

The songs began pouring out of him. He attacked the record industry and poked fun at how frightened everyone else was. One day Eminem caught wind of this wild gangster from Queens. He and Dr. Dre snapped him up straight away to the Aftermath record label. Within three years, 50 Cent had gone from rock bottom to a household name.

Dealing With Fear: *The Active Mode*

We're all too afraid. We don't want to offend a colleague, stir up conflict on the road, stand out from the crowd or take bold action. This fear lingers on from thousands of generations of evolution. So what can we do?

There are two ways of dealing with fear. Passive or active. A passive approach would be avoiding the situation that terrifies us at all costs and going for the safe and comfortable road in our daily lives. Whereas an active approach means embracing tough circumstances and repeatedly confronting fear. The choice is ours; we can choose to sit in comfort, or we can choose to be someone who welcomes the uncomfortable and faces fear head-on.

Nobody is born like this. Nobody instinctively goes the active route and embraces discomfort regularly. Fear is programmed into us and will always be riding shotgun. What separates some people is the will and hunger to rise above. Rather than being constantly on the defensive, the active types go looking for situations that will provoke a feeling of fear in them.

There is value in attacking life with a sense of boldness and urgency. Such a state brings a great sense of power.

Be Yourself

The most significant struggle people face is to simply be themselves. The passive types conform and become round pegs that fit perfectly into the crowd. But you get nowhere being that way. Nobody will pay attention to you if your energy stinks of weakness and timidity, which seems to be the default setting in human nature.

For 50 Cent, he overcame that struggle. Once he felt the power to show he didn't care about being like other people, his career turned around in remarkable fashion.

There really is only one thing we can control in this world: the attitude with which we respond to the circumstances around us. If we can overcome our anxieties and forge a fearless character, remarkable things start entering our lives.

The key to possessing supreme power is to assume the active mode in dealing with our fears. This means putting ourselves in situations we're afraid of. If we're scared, but we know it's going to be beneficial, we must do it anyway.

You can start today. If singing terrifies you, head to a karaoke night to get up on stage and let loose on *Mr Brightside* by The Killers. If you're single and you don't want to be, ask the cute barista for their number.

Most importantly, if you are afraid of doing something that is uniquely you, then you must do it. This means entering the arenas that we normally shy away from and making

LESSON 4 | *Fear*

the decisions we try to avoid. This gives you the power to change the direction of life. You'll notice that your fears are exaggerated, and confronting them brings you a new reality.

Lesson 5

boldness.

LESSON 5 | *Boldness*

Intellectually, you now know how to do a little mental jiu-jitsu to reframe fear. And while that will significantly reduce the fear you're feeling... it probably hasn't disappeared altogether. The final thing you need to overcome those fears is to give yourself a metaphorical kick in the ass. Pound your chest, and just go for it!

By embracing boldness, you can take action. Get out there. Tackle it head-on. Refuse to let fear hold you back.

If you confront your obstacles with an attitude of boldness, you might realise they quickly crumble away. What you thought was an unassailable mountain was really just a piddly little sandcastle after all.

Through three stories of bravery and determination across different domains, and discovering the four components of boldness, you'll be inspired to tackle any challenges you face by re-entering the world with newfound confidence.

LESSON 5 | *Boldness*

CHAPTER 13
Bold Mofo #1: *Richard Branson*

"If you opt for a safe life, you will never know what it's like to win."

Inspired by: **Screw It, Let's Do It,** *by Richard Branson*

The staff at Virgin have a name for their boss Richard Branson. They call him "Dr Yes." Bit of a weak nickname if you ask us, but there's a reason behind it - they call him this because he finds more reasons to *do* things than to *not* do them. His personal motto, whenever anyone asks him for something a little bizarre: *"Screw it. Let's do it!"*

He never says: *"I can't do this because I don't know how."* He will always give it a red hot crack. He values the ideas of his staff (no matter how crazy), and Virgin benefits from their hard work and drive toward achieving their own visions. He doesn't believe that a little word like *"can't"* should stop someone.

LESSON 5 | *Boldness*

If you don't have the right experience to reach your goal, look for another way in. If you haven't already achieved your vision, you may need to change. If you need to learn new skills and try new things, you can't let fear stop you.

By mixing a little boldness into our personal attitude cocktail, we can capitalise on opportunities that others are too timid to embrace. If you want to be a fashion designer, you don't have to go to art school - you can go and push a broom around the office of your favourite brand, keeping your eyes and ears open, always learning and looking for opportunities. If you want to be a writer, you don't need a degree - get in touch with authors and offer to be their research assistant. If you want to be a rapper, don't wait for a label to come and sign you - record your own music, sell it on the street, get it up on streaming platforms and start spreading the word.

With the right attitude, you can craftily find a way onto any ladder and start working your way up. This is the boldness with which Richard Branson has attacked his life. He started a little magazine when he was in high school and, through boldness, was able to get interviews with some of the world's biggest celebrities. Having never chartered a flight before, he used boldness to lease a plane and start Virgin Airlines. He was even bold enough to be the first billionaire to take a rocket ship to outer space. Having founded the Virgin Group in the 1970s, he now runs over 400 companies across all sorts of industries.

LESSON 5 | *Boldness*

Branson's First Money-Making Scheme

When Branson was nine years old, he came up with what he thought was an incredible idea: growing Christmas trees in his backyard. The seeds were cheap, and once he planted them, all he had to do was wait until they grew into trees before selling them at a ridiculous markup. The profit margins on the seeds were insane!

His first lesson in business was in figures and projections. Even though he was a dud in school and regularly failed maths tests, arithmetic seemed to make sense when he applied it to the real world of business. He bought a bag of 400 seeds for £5. If he sold each Christmas tree for just £2 each, he'd make £795 profit... that's a 16,000% ROI! He got his best mate Nik to come and plant seeds with him. They worked hard but had fun. Now all they needed to do was wait 18 months for the trees to grow, and they'd be rich.

His second lesson in business was... *money doesn't grow on trees!* As soon as a seedling popped up, a rabbit would come along and eat it. At this rate, they wouldn't have any trees left to sell.

His third lesson in business was to plan well but to be flexible. The Christmas tree idea looked like a bit of a flop, so they pivoted. Instead of growing trees, they went out shooting rabbits. These two nine-year-old kids were getting their revenge and also recouping their investment - they took the rabbits to the butcher and sold them for a few pennies each.

Ultimately, they got their money back and even made a small profit. They had fun and learnt a lot. Plus, all their family and friends got to eat some fresh rabbit pie.

While the original business didn't go according to plan, the boldness to have a crack set Branson on a trajectory toward success.

Student Magazine & Virgin Records

When Branson was in the middle of high school, around age 15, he started *Student* magazine. Everyone told him he was too young and inexperienced. They told him he couldn't do it... so he set out to prove them wrong.

He carefully calculated the costs for paper, ink, and printing, then worked out how much advertising revenue he'd need to cover the cost of the first edition. His mum gave him his first business loan - the £4 he needed to buy stamps to send letters. He sent letters to advertising executives to try and sell space; he sent letters to famous people trying to score interviews to be included in the magazine. Eventually, a couple of letters started coming back his way. He got his first cheque: £250 worth of advertising (which was enormous money for a young kid in the 1960s).

That year he generated a total of £8,000 in ad revenue but failed all his school exams. Branson had dyslexia, which made

LESSON 5 | *Boldness*

it difficult to learn in the same way most kids did. He saw no value in learning Latin or Advanced Calculus, so, at age 16, he decided to drop out of high school. He worked on *Student* magazine full time, working in his mate's basement during the day and drinking beer in the basement at night. He managed to secure interviews with some of the biggest names in the world, like Mick Jagger and John Lennon, names that even long-established magazines couldn't land. As well as boozing it up with celebs, the magazine had a serious side and sent reporters to cover global issues like the Vietnam War and the famine in Nigeria.

After establishing a bit of credibility and a loyal readership, Branson expanded his operations and started selling cut-priced records by mail order. He called it Virgin Mail Order, and the *Virgin* brand was born. When a nationwide mail strike halted this new venture, he had to find a way around it. He boldly strolled into a struggling local shoe shop and persuaded the owner to let him rent the back half of his shop and turn it into a record store. Branson made it a cool place for young people to come and listen to (and buy) music. He called it Virgin Records, and he soon outgrew the back of the shoe shop. Virgin Records expanded to a second store, then a third... and soon there was a Virgin Records store in almost every town.

LESSON 5 | *Boldness*

Branson hadn't even turned 20 yet, but that cash was flying in faster than he could count it. A seed had been planted[27], and now he wanted to create an empire.

Virgin Airlines

After finding such success in *selling* records, Branson started *making* them. By 1977, Virgin Records had a handful of successful artists in their stable, and Branson went on an international signing spree looking for undiscovered talent. He travelled the world looking for 'hidden gems' (AKA no names he could sign cheaply, then try to make big with a small budget). By the end of his trip, he was cooked, so on the final leg of the journey, he invited a lady friend for a bit of rest and relaxation[28] in Jamaica and Puerto Rico with him.

When they got to the Jamaican airport, they found that their flight had been cancelled. People were roaming around, looking lost. No one was doing anything... so Branson boldly took action. He chartered a small private 50-seater plane for $2,000. Then he wrote up a sign: *"Virgin Airways... Single Flight to Puerto Rico - $39."*

Branson had never chartered a plane before, but he saw an opportunity and took action to seize it (at this stage, it was mostly the opportunity to get laid, but there was also an

---

[27] Much like his Christmas Tree venture... I wonder if it's a coincidence that he planted 400 literal seeds and now has sprouted 400 businesses from metaphorical seeds.

[28] I guess "rest and relaxation" was the "Netflix and chill" before Netflix came along.

opportunity for a new business venture lurking somewhere beneath the sultry surface). As you know today, *Virgin Airlines* has become much more than just a single opportunistic flight. Eventually, they served dozens of countries worldwide and later splintered off divisions like Virgin Australia, Virgin Europe, Virgin Nigeria and Virgin America.

Perhaps an even more substantial opportunity that grew out of that inaugural flight was *Virgin Galactic*. When Branson wrote his first autobiography in 1998, this was just a vision, another way for him to have a crack at a new challenge and have some fun along the way. He wanted to offer space flights to the general public. No one else was doing it. Fast forward to 2021, and he did it! Branson was the first billionaire up in space. He beat his rival billionaire buddies Jeff Bezos and Elon Musk to the punch. Branson flew into space in June 2021, with Musk's SpaceX a few months behind the curve, taking their first flight of civilian tourists up in September.

In 35 years, Branson and Virgin Airlines grew from renting one plane to initiating space travel.

Branson the Bold

Richard Branson is, without a doubt, a bold mofo. In addition to these impressive business ventures, he also broke records in speed boats and flew a hot air balloon across the Atlantic. The ultimate lesson from Branson is not that you have to build a mega business and do wild shit in your personal life

LESSON 5 | *Boldness*

to be successful. No, Branson's most important lesson is this: if there's something you really want to do, get out there and do it.

His *Student* magazine was very small at first. He sold ad space from a payphone at school because he believed it would work. And that was the start of something special. Whatever your goal is, you won't succeed unless you let go of your fears, welcome change and embrace boldness. Get out there and make it happen.

LESSON 5 | *Boldness*

CHAPTER 14
Bold Mofo #2: *David Goggins*

"You are stopping you. You are giving up instead of getting hard."

Inspired by: **Can't Hurt Me,** *by David Goggins*

Do you know who you really are?
　Do you know what you're really capable of?
　Probably not.
　And you're not alone.

In every town, in every city, in every country around the world, people are mindlessly wandering the streets, completely unaware of their true potential. We're like dead-eyed zombies roaming the streets, addicted to safety, staying tightly tucked in our comfort zones, and not wanting to change or face our fears.

　David Goggins used to be one of them. He was dealt a bad hand - he was born broken, grew up with beatdowns, was tormented at school and copped overt racism more times than he could count. Goggins was poor, surviving on welfare, living in government subsidy housing, and had smothering depression. He lived life at the bottom of the barrel. His future forecast ranged somewhere between 'miserably grim,' 'bleak as fuck,' or 'complete tragedy.'

But Goggins knew that no self-help book would offer him anything more than a temporary band-aid, no motivation hack was going to rewire his brain, and no mentor was going to come along and drag him by the scruff of the neck back to the surface. He realised that if he wanted to claw his way out from the bottom of the barrel and take the bad hand he'd been dealt by life and turn it into something salvageable, it was his problem to fix alone.

So, Goggins did away with the same comfortable choices he'd been making his whole life. He scrapped the decisions that had been slowly killing him, the ones that had led him to be overweight, undereducated and unworthy... and instead, he sought pain and challenges. He "fell in love with suffering," and eventually, he "transformed from the weakest piece of shit on the planet into one of the hardest motherfuckers[29] God ever created."

Odds are, you had a better childhood than Goggins. But no matter who you are, who your parents were, where you

---

[29] Self-anointed, but probably pretty accurate when you hear about some of the wild shit he got up to.

live, what you do for a living, or how much money you have - you're probably only living at 40% capacity. Maybe less.

Heraclitus, a philosopher born in the Persian empire in the 5th century BC, once said: *"Out of every one hundred men, 10 shouldn't even be here, 80 are just targets. 9 are real fighters, and we are lucky to have them. Ah, but one, one is the warrior."* If you want to be that warrior, you can be. But you're going to have to be bold.

The Accountability Mirror

In high school, Goggins went out of his way to piss people off by becoming the exact stereotype that racist white people loathed and feared. He sagged his pants low beneath his ass, rigged up some serious speakers to his car and rolled around the neighbourhood, blasting Snoop Dog and NWA. He even had fuzzy dice hanging on the rearview mirror. No one expected anything of him, so he did everything he could to live down to those expectations. Everything he did was to goad people and get a reaction.

On the surface, he acted tough. But deep down, he was in real pain. Goggins realised he was living a shallow life - he had no vision and no chance of any kind of success. But he did have a dream: to enter the air force.

One night, after his shower, he got out and wiped the steam from the bathroom mirror. He took a good, hard look

LESSON 5 | *Boldness*

at himself... and didn't like who was staring back. He was a low-budget thug with no purpose and no future.

Goggins felt so disgusted at who was staring back in the mirror that he wanted to punch the reflection in the glass. But instead, Goggins started lecturing him. He got real:

> *"Look at you. Why do you think the air force wants your punk ass? You are one dumb mother fucker. You read like a third-grader. You're a fucking joke! You never tried hard at anything in your life besides basketball. No one in the military sags their pants. They don't talk like a wannabe gangster. Yeah, I know shit is fucked up. I know what you've been through. I was there bitch! Merry fucking Christmas. Now suck it up and get at it!"*

By the time he was done talking, he looked different. He stood up a little straighter. He had a different aura about him.

A new ritual was born. This initial spontaneous venting session altered the trajectory of his life, so this exercise became something he continued to carry out for years. He used it when he needed to get his grades up, when he needed to get in shape, or when he was applying to the airforce.

This is what Goggins calls the "Accountability Mirror." We can do it too. Every day, you take a look in the mirror and hold yourself accountable to the goals you set to see if you're

LESSON 5 | *Boldness*

on the Slight Edge path to fulfilling your vision. Nobody likes to hear the hard truth. Individually and as a culture, we avoid what we need to hear the most. So there is a great opportunity if you can become one of the rare few that can handle a little self-directed brutality.

If your finances are a mess, don't say that you need to tighten up your budget a little. Be honest - you're broke! If you've worked for 30 years doing the same shit you've hated day in and day out because you were afraid to quit and take a risk, don't tell yourself that things will get better soon. Tell it like it is - you've been living like a wimp! If you look in the mirror and see a fat person, don't tell yourself to lose a couple of pounds. Tell the truth - you're fat! You've wasted enough time. You're not living up to your vision. Something needs to change.

The mirror will tell you the truth every time... so stop lying to yourself. One path is to treat yourself kindly in those few minutes of looking in the mirror, and you'll guarantee that you stay the same. The alternative is to be bold, tell yourself the truth, objectively call yourself out... and you might be able to initiate change.

Truth avoidance is a major problem in our society today, along with a myriad of other outside forces. Goggins realised that while these external factors made life more challenging, they weren't holding him back; it was his inability to be brutally honest with himself and face the truth. If you think something or someone is stopping you, the mirror has got news for you: it's not the world that's stopping you - *you* are stopping you.

There's no more time to waste. Hours and days evaporate like creeks in a desert. That's why it's ok to be cruel to yourself as long as you realise you're doing it to become better. We all need thicker skin to improve in life. Being precious when we look in the mirror isn't going to inspire the change we need to shift our present and open our future.

The morning after Goggins did that first accountability mirror, he ditched the fuzzy dice. He tucked in his shirt, wore his pants with a belt, and stopped eating crap for lunch. For the first time, being liked and acting cool was a waste of his time. Instead of eating with the popular kids, he found his own table and ate alone. Instead of living down to the expectations society placed on a black teenager from a broken home, he started living up to his own vision.

Pushing To New Limits: *The 40% Rule*

Goggins pushed himself to what he thought was his limit. He'd been through Navy SEAL training, he'd survived Hell Week, and he was training with some of the hardest warriors on the planet. When the sign-up sheet for the San Diego 100-mile ultramarathon was passed around, he thought, 'what the hell' and popped his name down.

LESSON 5 | *Boldness*

By the time the race rolled around, he hadn't run more than a mile in over six months. He'd been purely doing strength training and powerlifting to harden his body. But he figured 'how hard can it be' - all he had to do was finish 100 miles in 24 hours. That's only 15 minutes per mile - if he was pooped, he could walk and still make the time required.

He knew if he paced himself, he could get there. But Goggins isn't a man that paces himself. As soon as the starter's gun went off, he bolted. Plus, it probably didn't help that one of his SEAL buddies had egged him on the night before to pump some iron. His mate set the challenge, saying: *"You know Goggins, when the Vikings were getting ready to raid a fucking village, and they were camped out in the woods in their tents, do you think they were sitting around the campfire and drinking herbal tea?!?"* So his body was already feeling it from a night of lifting weights and drinking alcohol, plus he weighed a very un-marathon-like 270 pounds at this point.

By the time he hit the 40-mile mark, his kidneys had failed, and he'd broken all the small bones in his feet. On top of this, he suffered dual stress fractures in his lower legs, so he wrapped his feet and ankles in compression tape in an attempt to stave off the agony. The course was a one-mile loop you completed 100 laps of. After his 40th lap, with no training and poor preparation, this was his reward: pissing blood, shins on fire, and his lungs seizing. With every lap, he

LESSON 5 | *Boldness*

returned to the question: *"Why the fuck are you still doing this to yourself?"*

We tend to set our vision and hatch our grand plans for our life when we've got food, water, and comfort. We hatch our biggest dreams and set our challenging goals when we're sitting on a beanbag in front of the fireplace with a barista-made almond piccolo in our hands. Everything seems doable when we're in that soft environment. When we actually start making change, it takes boldness to keep pushing beyond what we think our limit is. When we're peeing metaphorical blood as we chase our goals, when our metaphorical lungs are seizing, and we feel like we can't go on, when our metaphorical shins are crumbling with every stride, and we just want to sit down and have a lemonade... that's when we need boldness to keep nudging ourselves forward.

Once we've given it a red hot crack, and we think we've maxed out, when we think we've hit our limit, it's time to ask ourselves an important question: *"What am I capable of?"* We habitually settle for less than our best: at work, in school, in our relationships and on the playing field. We settle as individuals, and we teach our children to settle for less than their best. This eventually ripples out. It merges and multiplies within our communities and society as a whole, and it ultimately breeds a general culture of mediocrity.

LESSON 5 | Boldness

Goggins is a wild man, constantly trying to find his *actual* limit. Not the point where his mind is asking him to chill the fuck out and take a break. But the point where his body actually packs it in. And although he's come close, he still hasn't found that limit. He wants to prove to himself and to all of us that we're capable of accomplishing more than we ever thought possible.

Goggins found that the point at which our brain is begging us to stop is only 40% of our potential. When you're trying to write that book you always wanted to write, and you've written a few shitty chapters, and your brain is telling you to give up - you've still got 60% left in the tank to keep pushing. When you're trying to start a business, and you keep hitting brick walls, and you're ready to throw in the towel - you still have 60% left in the tank. Or when you're running an ultramarathon, and your body is praying that you stop - you've still got 60% left in the tank.

When Goggins was ready to curl into the foetal position and stay there for a month or two after he'd finished his 40th lap, he remembered *The 40% Rule* and knew he still had more to give.

He eventually finished that 100-mile race. And because he still had time on the clock, he decided to do an extra lap just to remind himself that he was a seriously bold mofo. When he collapsed at the finish line, he was taken straight to the emergency room. His wife was crying and shouting at him

LESSON 5 | *Boldness*

through his delirious haze, berating him for being so stupid and pushing himself this hard. Those hundred one-mile laps were harder than Hell Week, more challenging than his deployment to Iraq, and it showed him that his whole life, he'd been selling himself short. He always had more left in the tank. Even when he thought he'd hit his limit, there was still more he could give.

And so can you.

When we think we've hit our limit, we're really only at the 40% mark. *The 40% Rule* can be applied to anything because nothing in life turns out as we hope. There are always challenges. We will all be tempted to walk away from commitments, give up on goals and dreams and sell our own happiness short at some point. We may feel empty with no more to give when really, we haven't tapped into even half of the treasure buried deep in our minds, hearts and souls. If you keep pushing through, you'll uncover a whole new side of you, a previously hidden pool of potential you've never harnessed. You're not going to go from 40 to 100 on your first go, but by constantly pushing beyond your perceived limit, you'll add a couple of percentage points each time. And eventually, by being bold enough to keep challenging yourself, you might one day realise what you're *really* capable of.

LESSON 5 | *Boldness*

CHAPTER 15
Bold Mofo #3: *Malala Yousafzai*

"I told myself, Malala, you have already faced death. This is your second life. Don't be afraid — if you are afraid, you can't move forward."

Inspired by: **I Am Malala,** *by Malala Yousafzi*

When Malala Yousafzi was born in Pakistan, nobody congratulated her parents. *"I was a girl in a land where rifles are fired in celebration of a son, while daughters are hidden away behind a curtain; their role in life is simply to prepare food, clean the home, and give birth to children,"* she said.

She grew up playing cricket with her younger brother, as well as some local neighbourhood kids. There were five in total, two girls and three boys. But while they were all together when they were young children, the girls knew that as they got older, they would eventually be expected to stay inside rather than have fun playing in the streets. The two daughters would be expected to cook and serve their brothers and fathers.

LESSON 5 | *Boldness*

Boys and men could roam freely about town, but women and girls could not go out without a male relative to accompany them. If her mother went out, she would at least need to take her 5-year-old son with her since their predominantly patriarchal society determined women could not look after themselves.

Malala had decided early on that she would not be like that. Her father always said to her and to anyone who would listen: *"Malala will be free as a bird."* But as she watched her brothers running across the rooftops, flying their kites and skillfully flicking the strings back and forth to cut each other down, she wondered how free a girl in her country could ever be.

Malala's Parents

Toor Pekai, Malala's mother, started going to school when she was a young girl. But at age six, with less than a semester of schooling under her belt, she stopped. Her father and brothers encouraged her to go to school, but she was the only girl in a class full of boys. She claimed that she was smarter than the boys and would proudly carry her school books in her backpack, but every morning she left her girl cousins who got to stay home and play instead. She was envious. There seemed to be no point in going to school if she would end up cooking, cleaning, and bringing up children anyway - so one

LESSON 5 | *Boldness*

day, she sold her books, used the money to buy some lollies, and never went back.

It was only when she met Ziauddin, Malala's father, that she regretted her decision. As an educated and well-read man, he spent time writing her love poems she sadly couldn't read herself. Malala's father thought there was nothing more important than knowledge and learning, so even though he had no money and no connections, it had been his lifelong dream to start his own school.

The school he attended as a kid in his village was just a small building with no flooring or toilets. Most classes were taught outside under a tree, and if nature called, you had to head out to the field to do your business. But his sisters weren't allowed to go to school, so he felt lucky to have been given the gift of education.

Ziauddin believed the lack of education was the root of all of Pakistan's problems. Ignorance allowed politicians to fool people into re-electing bad administrations. He believed school was something that should be accessible to all - rich and poor, boys and girls. The school of his dreams would have desks and chairs, a library, computers, bright posters on the walls, and, importantly - toilets. He hated the way most schools rewarded obedience over creativity and open-mindedness, so his school would encourage independent thought.

LESSON 5 | *Boldness*

Malala's Early Schooling

Malala's father had started the school of his dreams, and it was going well. After starting their first day with just three pupils, they'd grown to over 800 students and expanded to a *second* school campus.

By the age of seven, Malala was used to being top of her class, often helping out fellow students if they had any problems with their schoolwork. She was known for participating in everything - badminton, drama, cricket, art, and even singing (although she was no good at it).

But tensions soon started to rise. There was a new bloke in town - he called himself a Mufti, an authority on Islamic law. The self-proclaimed Mufti had been watching girls going in and out of school every day and became angry, particularly as some of the girls were teenagers and, according to Islam, should be staying home.

The Mufti went to the woman who owned the property the school was on and said: *"Ziauddin is running a HARAM school in your building and bringing shame on the neighbourhood."* He continued: *"These girls should be in purdah[30]. Take this school off him, and I will create my own school in its place to teach Islam. If you do this, I will pay you more now, plus you will get a reward in the next world for helping spread the teaching of Allah."* The landlord refused and went straight to Malala's father, telling him the Mufti was starting a campaign against

---

[30] Full headdresses and face coverings.

him. She said she would not give the school over to him but that he needed to be careful not to incite further action.

One night, after the Mufti had failed to persuade the landlady to cancel the school's lease, he gathered some of the elders and influential people from around the neighbourhood and rolled up to Malala's door. The Mufti confronted Ziauddin by saying: *"I am representing good Muslims from around the world, and we all think your girls' school is haram and blasphemy. You should close it. Girls should not be going to school."* The mufti said: *"There are men in the reception, and they see girls enter the school... this is very bad. A girl is so sacred she should be in purdah."*

Malala's father retorted: *"I have a solution - the school has another gate; the girls will enter through the side gate so men cannot see them."* The Mufti clearly wasn't happy because he wanted the school closed altogether, but the elders accepted the compromise.

Everyone left, and all was settled... for now.

The Taliban Arrives

The Taliban made their way from Afghanistan across into Pakistan and started controlling towns and villages near Malala's home. The local leader, Sufi Mohammad, proclaimed there should be no more education for women or girls in

LESSON 5 | Boldness

Pakistan. He said on the radio: *"If someone can show any example in history where Islam allows females in school, they can come and piss on my beard.[31]"* The Taliban radio show began shit-talking school administrators and congratulating girls by name who left school: *"Miss So-and-so has stopped going to school and will go to heaven... Miss X of Village Y has stopped education at Class 5, and she is to be congratulated."* The girls who kept going to school, like Malala, were referred to as buffaloes and sheep. But she and her friends couldn't understand what was wrong; they just wanted to go to school. Tensions continued to rise, with the Taliban trying to wrestle power and the Pakistani army trying to push back and eject them from the country entirely. For the young girls, school was something of a haven, a way to escape the violence and shooting going on in the streets of their hometowns. Soon schools were under threat too. The radio messages weren't enough to stop girls from going to school, so the Taliban stepped it up a notch. They started bombing schools. Initially, they were bombing schools at night when no one was there, starting with the all-girls schools. Then more and more schools were bombed across the country, and the explosions were getting closer and closer to Malala's hometown of Mingora.

---

[31] He must've been pretty confident to put his neck (beard) on the line like that.

LESSON 5 | *Boldness*

Malala's father hated the fact that most people would not speak up, so he wrote a letter to the local newspaper condemning the actions of the Taliban. He wrote: *"Please don't harm my children because the God you believe in is the same God they pray to every day. You can take my life, but please don't kill my schoolchildren."* Many people called to congratulate him for his boldness, saying that he had cast the first stone into a still pond, and the ripples of impact were starting to spread. Thanks to him, they felt more courage to speak up themselves.

From that moment on, he kept a poem in his pocket written by Martin Niemöller, who had lived in Nazi Germany:

First, they came for the communists, and I didn't speak out because I wasn't a communist.
Then they came for the socialists, and I didn't speak out because I wasn't a socialist.
Then they came for the trade unionists, and I didn't speak out because I wasn't a trade unionist.

LESSON 5 | *Boldness*

Then they came for the Jews, and I didn't speak out because I was not a Jew.
Then they came for the Catholics, and I didn't speak out because I was not a Catholic.
Then they came for me, and there was no one left to speak for me.

When Malala started school, there were 27 girls in her class, but by the start of January 2009, only ten girls were remaining. A few had left their town to find a place outside of the Taliban's reach, but many had heeded the warnings and decided to stay home and not be educated. The Taliban had given a hard deadline: girls must stop going to school by the end of the semester.

How could they stop more than 50,000 girls from attending school in the twenty-first century? Malala kept hoping something would happen so that schools could remain open. But the deadline kept creeping towards them, and nothing had changed. Her school was determined to be the last bell to stop ringing, but eventually, they too succumbed to the demands and locked the school doors.

Malala Speaks Up

While a few brave men were speaking out against the regime, Malala knew that the best person to speak out was someone who was directly impacted by the ban on schooling. *If one man can destroy everything, why can't one girl change it?*

No other girls were willing to speak up - either they were scared (understandable), or their parents wouldn't allow them (also understandable). So Malala took it upon herself to be bold. She did an interview for a local television station. Then more media were keen to tell her story - TV, radio, newspapers, and magazines. The more interviews she gave, the stronger she felt and the more the cause to get girls back to school was supported. At only eleven years old, she spoke with the power and confidence of someone much older.

While she acted tough on the surface, she also admitted she was scared that if the Taliban caught her in school uniform or with school books, they would throw acid on her face like they had done to girls in Afghanistan. She cried because she didn't want to stop learning. Malala felt that by losing her schooling, she was losing her future. The opportunity that came with education was everything to her - an opportunity to live her life differently than her mother, aunties, and grandmother before her. The Taliban could stop her from going to school, but they couldn't stop her mind from thinking and learning. All she wanted to do was go to school and have a chance.

LESSON 5 | *Boldness*

People often said the Taliban might kill her father, but not Malala. *"Malala is a child,"* they would say, *"and even the Taliban wouldn't try to kill a child."*

October 9th, 2012

Initially, the Taliban had a blanket ban on all girls attending school. But due to the public pressure brought about by ongoing media campaigns, they lifted this to allow girls up to Grade 4 to return to school. Malala and her friends were in Grade 5, but they pretended to be younger to sneak back to school secretly.

A Pakistani journalist visited Malala at her family home to interview her about how she felt about her boldness playing a role in enabling girls to return to school. After asking her first few questions, the journalist became very emotional. She turned to Ziauddin and asked: *"Did you know that the Taliban have threatened this innocent girl?"* They had no idea what this woman was talking about, but a quick google search uncovered a new video that had emerged that morning of the Taliban issuing a threat against Shad Begum, a 33-year-old social worker and activist, and against Malala. Initially, they didn't take the threat seriously, but family and friends from across the country began calling them to issue stern warnings for Malala to keep her head down.

LESSON 5 | *Boldness*

The day everything changed was Tuesday, 9 October 2012. Malala was just finishing her exams for the school year, and she and her friends were hanging around at school chatting about how they went before getting the late bus home.

When the bus arrived, all the kids ran down the steps and piled in. The other girls all covered their faces before leaving the building, whereas Malala wore a scarf over her head but never over her face.

All the girls were singing and chatting. Since they were in the back of the bus, they couldn't see what was happening on the road in front of them. A young bearded man stepped out and waved the bus down. *"Is this the Khushal School Bus?"* he asked the driver[32]. When the man asked for information about some of the school students, the driver basically told him to buzz off and go to the school office if he had more questions.

As they spoke, a second young man dressed in white approached the back of the van. *"Look, it's one of those journalists coming to ask for an interview,"* said one of Malala's friends. But this young man didn't look like a journalist. He swung himself into the van and leaned in.

"Who is Malala?" he demanded.

No one spoke a word, but a few girls glanced over to see that Malala was the only one without her face covered. That's when he lifted up a black Colt 45 pistol.

---

[32] The driver thought it was a pretty stupid question since "Khushal School Bus" was written on the side of the vehicle.

Some of the girls screamed. The gunman fired three shots, one after another. The first went through Malala's left eye socket. She slumped forward and fell into her friend's lap. The second and third shots hit the girls on either side of her. The bus driver sped toward the hospital.

Boldness Beats Cowardice

A week after the shooting, after multiple rounds of major surgeries in three hospitals across two countries, Malala eventually woke up. She was in Birmingham, UK - thousands of miles away from home, with no idea where her family was and a tube in her neck to help her breathe.

Malala was bold. She was speaking up for her basic right to go to school. She risked her comfort and safety to stand up for what she believed in, and to stand for the 50,000 girls who were banned from going to school.

The gunman was the opposite of bold. He was cowardly. He tried to shoot an innocent 15-year-old girl in cold blood just to keep her quiet. He thought if he killed Malala, he was serving his own cause.

But it backfired. All the Taliban had done was make Malala's campaign global. Britain's former Prime Minister, Gordon Brown, started a movement called 'I Am Malala' with

LESSON 5 | *Boldness*

a global petition to demand no child be denied schooling by 2015. Beyoncé wrote Malala a card and posted a photo of it on Facebook, Selena Gomez tweeted about the incident, and Madonna dedicated a song. Malala's favourite actress and activist, Angelina Jolie, also sent a message.

We often don't realise how powerful an act of boldness can be. Some people choose boldness; others choose cowardice. It seems statistically impossible, but a coward fires three shots from point-blank range at three girls in a van and they all survive. A coward's bullet hits a bold girl. It swells her brain and severs her facial nerve in a split second. But a split second later, millions of people around the globe begin spreading her message.

We can agree that Malala is one of the boldest mofos of them all; she channelled her fear into a cause worth fighting for and interpreted her close call with death as a reason to fight harder. Boldness exists within all of us. It exists within you. Letting fear hold you back from a powerful act of boldness might not only limit your potential, but could stop you from inspiring those around you too.

Your vision may not spark a global movement or end the patriarchy, but it might just change your life. If that means embracing boldness and kicking fear to the curb, then take

LESSON 5 | *Boldness*

this as your sign to switch your attitude. It is time to make a stand for what you want. It is time to be bold.

LESSON 5 | *Boldness*

CHAPTER 16
Components of Boldness

"The fear you feel is a sign. If courage is never required in your life, you're living a boring life. Put yourself in a position that demands you take a leap."

Inspired by: **Courage Is Calling,** *by Ryan Holiday*

You've now read the stories of three seriously bold individuals. Branson is bold in the work and business sense, Goggins is bold in the physical sense, and Malala is bold in the moral sense. You might not want to start 400 businesses or run 100 miles or speak out against an oppressive regime, but whatever you want to do will require a modicum of boldness. To conquer fear so we can learn new things that allow us to change in some way that supports our vision, we'll need to be bold.

There is nothing we prize more than boldness, yet these days, nothing seems in shorter supply. But boldness is not like a precious gemstone that takes a billion years of pressure and energy to create. Nor is it like oil that must be drawn from deep

LESSON 5 | *Boldness*

underground. Boldness is not a finite resource only available to an elite few. No, boldness is something much simpler. It is renewable. It is in each of us. Every day. Everywhere we go. It's something that we are capable of at a moment's notice in matters big and small, physical and moral. There are daily opportunities to put it to use.

And yet it remains so rare... Because we are afraid. Because it's easier not to get involved. Because we have something else we're working on. Because now is not a good time. We'd rather stick to our comfort zone and keep doing what feels safe.

The logic is understandable - it's easier NOT to be bold. But if *everyone* took the easy way out, what's left?

The greatest moments in human history all share one thing. Whether it's starting a business, running an ultramarathon, or going to school when you've been threatened not to - the thing they have in common is the *boldness* of ordinary people. People who did what needed to be done. People who decided to take responsibility. People who said: *"If not me, then who? If not now, when?"*

The next time you see an easy path, take the hard route instead. It's going to require you to be bold - if it were easy, boldness wouldn't be required. The next time you choose to take ownership and assert agency over your own fate instead of waiting for someone else to come and save you, the following four components of boldness will come in handy.

Boldness Component #1: *Prepare*

'Training' is not reserved for athletes and soldiers; it is available to all. Preparation is the key to overcoming fear in any situation. If something new comes unexpectedly around the corner and we're unprepared, of course we'll struggle to overcome it. But the things we anticipate and prepare for become easy to confront. As Epictetus said, whenever we face adversity, our goal should be to say: *"This is what I've trained for."*

We're talking about *practice*. With practice, we go through the actions in our minds. We build the muscle memory of what we do in situations like these. We practise scales, so our fingers are ready to tackle that epic new piece. Good luck playing Chopin's *Fantasie-Impromptu* on piano or Vivaldi's *Four Seasons* on the violin without some serious finger dexterity built over years (or decades) of practice.

Get comfortable with discomfort. Get someone to ask you tough questions deliberately. Get familiar with anything they could possibly throw at you. Work out with a weight vest on, play the guitar blindfolded, and kick a footy with your opposite foot. Do it a thousand times (then a thousand more) when there is no pressure so that when the real test comes, you'll know exactly what you need to do.

Knowledge helps. Understanding what needs to be done might be the first step. But it is rigorous preparation that makes you bold when it's time to shine.

LESSON 5 | *Boldness*

Boldness Component #2: *Decide*

Often, *deciding* is the most important part of a job, yet it's the thing we're most afraid to do. Making a decision means choosing one thing and rejecting another. We'd much rather try to keep both doors open as long as possible. But sooner or later, if we don't choose, the choice will be made for us... and it probably won't be the one we want.

Anne Mulcahy stepped into Xerox as the new Chief Executive Officer in 2001. She'd inherited a company in more than a little bit of trouble. They'd just come off the back of a $273M loss the year before, the debt-to-equity ratio cracked 900%, and Moody's rated its bonds as 'junk.' Plus, the share price had dropped 92% in two years, wiping out $38B of shareholder value. And, to cap it all off, the government had just launched an investigation into its accounts.

With $19B in debt and only $100M in cash, Mulcahy described the situation as "terrifying" (probably an understatement). She decided that the job of a CEO was to be a *decider*, someone who made the hard calls no one else was bold enough to make. So, she started making decisions.

Mulcahy didn't take a weekend off for two years. She shut down a number of businesses, including the inkjet printer unit that she'd championed earlier in her career. She cut $2.5B out of Xerox's cost structure. Of course, none of these decisions were easy, but they were necessary to give

LESSON 5 | *Boldness*

the company a fighting chance, a flicker of hope to stave off utter catastrophe.

In the two years before Mulcahy stepped in, 2000 and 2001, the company's losses totalled $367M. By 2006, Xerox posted profits in excess of $1B and sported a much stronger balance sheet. In 2008, Anne Mulcahy was named "Chief Executive of the Year" by *Chief Executive* magazine, having guided the company through a 7-year rebuild to reclaim its dominance.

Being the decider is hard work. The doctor in the operating room cannot delay: they must make decisions quickly, they must act and have the courage to face the life-and-death results of the performance. The same goes for the firefighter, the trader, the performer, and the leader - nothing is gained from being timid. Boldness is required around every corner.

We lie to ourselves and say we need more time or more data or more research, or more debate and deliberation to make the right decision. But really, we're just finding ways to delay. We don't want to have to own the consequences. Some famous person[33] said: *"Whatever you're not changing, you're choosing."* By not quitting that job, by not leaving that relationship, by not making that investment, by not standing up for what we believe in - we're choosing the alternate path.

---

[33] Probably Mark Twain or Abraham Lincoln or Henry Ford (or maybe just some bloke from the pub).

Even though you tell yourself you're just taking more time to decide, really - you've already decided. You've decided to keep things exactly the way they are. *Not* choosing is, in fact, still a choice. And a poor one at that. It's much better to be intentional, boldly standing behind one option over the other rather than passively receiving whatever is already coming our way.

The best time to have tackled a hard problem and made a bold decision was a long time ago. The second best time is now.

Boldness Component #3: *Act*

In France, they have a term: *petites actions*. It's all about taking those first few small steps, making that first little bit of progress and using that initial inching forward to help build momentum into substantial action. Like how the wiggle of a pinky finger can get you up off the couch or how writing a single sentence can lead to a whole chapter. Whenever we feel afraid in the face of some enormous problem, it helps to break it into *petites actions* and start doing little things that will eventually add up. Often the best place to start isn't some death-defying stunt, but rather the small and simple first crack in the armour.

We might think that small steps won't lead to anything important, but the Slight Edge showed us the power of consistent positive progress. On the path to our grand vision, we make one small change, the thing that is right in front of us... then we can figure out what to do next. Eliminate one problem, send one email, or write one paragraph. Get that first spark that may eventually lead to a roaring fire.

Your headlights shine on just a few metres of a dark road in front of you, but those few metres of light are enough to get you safely all the way home. Once you make that first inch of progress, the next small step becomes obvious. It's easy to be paralysed by fear, but it takes boldness to take some kind of action - *any* action that gets you closer to your vision, no matter how small.

There's no way around it; if you want to make progress, you must take action.

Boldness Component #4: *Inspire*

One person's timid act spreads like a virus, infecting those around them. Fear is contagious. But so is boldness.

When I (Ashto) am on the footy field, and a teammate goes in hard at a contest, you start to stand a little taller. When someone crashes a pack, lays a massive tackle, or puts in a strong shepherd to block an opponent and create space for a teammate - that boldness infects the rest of the team. All it takes is for one person to be bold in service of the team's grand vision, and suddenly everyone feels and acts a little bolder too.

LESSON 5 | *Boldness*

When another country called on Sparta for military help, the Spartans wouldn't send their entire army - they sent just *one* Spartan commander. The country that asked for help was probably feeling a bit jibbed, expecting the Spartan army to come and rescue them; then they see a lone bloke strolling over the hill... but this was all it took. The Spartan's boldness and courage on the battlefield was enough to infect and inspire all those around him.

One person who knows what they're doing, who isn't afraid, who has a plan. One person who is prepared, who decides, who takes action. That is enough to reinforce an outnumbered army, buck a trend, calm the chaos, and generate real change.

YOU can be that one person that inspires your whole team in whatever domain you're operating. You don't need to be the smartest or the biggest or the fittest or the most well-connected; you just need to be bold.

Conclusion

take your turn.

CONCLUSION | *Take Your Turn*

So where does all of this leave us?

When Ashto and I prepare our podcast notes for the book we're reading and reviewing that week, we have a section for a 'meta capper.' This is our own inside jargon where we're basically asking ourselves: *"What is the* actual *point of this book?"* We've trawled the depths of Vision, Change, Learning, Fear and Boldness... so what is the one thing that ties them all together?

The meta capper of Attitude: *It's your turn, so take it.*

Your turn to speak up, to stand out, to build a following, to market a product, to make a connection, to solve an interesting problem. Your turn to write, sing, invent, create, ask a question, launch a project, organise a protest, open the door for someone, question authority, make a short film, direct, produce, create, or adopt. To learn a new skill, to help someone who needs you... to be missed if you're gone.

It's easy, it's fun, and it's guaranteed to work. Of course you can do it. All of that is true... except for the part about fun, easy and guaranteed.

This might not work. It might not be fun. We hope you'll do it anyway.

CHAPTER 17
Take Your Turn

"Every interaction, every moment when it's your turn, is an opportunity."

> Inspired by: **What To Do When It's Your Turn (And It's Always Your Turn),** *by Seth Godin*

Two hot-shot executives are on an escalator[34]. They're suited up, carrying briefcases, looking all important, and already a little rushed and agitated as they're very busy people on their way to do something they think is very important. Suddenly, with a lurch, the escalator comes to a halt. Both executives are now trapped on a broken escalator, apparently unable to get to where they want to go.

The first sighs in frustration, while the second starts calling for help. Here are important, busy people, unable to get to safety because the escalator has broken and no one has come to save them.

---

[34] Check out this funny video: youtube.com/watch?v=VQVnx2KERvw (or search "stuck on an escalator" on YouTube).

CONCLUSION | *Take Your Turn*

Too many people today are unable to see that all you have to do is start walking up. The steps are already there; they're part of the escalator. Sure - they're not as easy or automatic or convenient as a functioning escalator... but walking up the stairs sure as hell beats being stuck.

What are the broken escalators in your life? What things require fixing, that you're waiting for someone else to come and do for you? Really - all you need to do is tap into your initiative and start putting one foot in front of the other.

Pick Yourself

Usually, when we hear, "it's your turn," it means we've been picked. We're the next one who is being given an opportunity, the next plant manager, the next in line for a promotion, the next person in line at the deli. This is the model we're most familiar with, the one where we wait for change to happen to us.

A better model of "your turn" is the model of the person who *makes* change. Rather than sitting around waiting to be called upon, we can make the choice to choose ourselves, to look in the accountability mirror and say: "it's your turn." Your turn to choose the change that is interesting, change for the better, change that connects us, and most importantly, change in service of our vision.

CONCLUSION | *Take Your Turn*

No one is coming to pick you. No one is coming to say: "You've made it; you've waited long enough; your time is now." That's on you. You must give yourself permission to start making changes. The only way to get your turn is to take it for yourself.

The Person Who Fails The Most, Wins

Writer and researcher Dan McGinn once conducted an experiment. He got a computer keyboard that used to belong to Malcolm Gladwell[35]. I guess the idea was that if you could use the keyboard that Malcolm Gladwell used, you might be able to write a little more like Gladwell (and hopefully achieve similar commercial success along with it).

This idea is kind of like asking a successful person where they get all their good ideas from. This is a pretty unhelpful question. A far better question would be to ask: *"Where do you get all of your BAD ideas from?"* Because if you have enough bad ideas, you'll have absolutely no trouble finding some winners. That's what successful people do - they let the ideas flow wildly. They get to work and let the ideas come to them.

Note: they don't wait for ideas to come and *then* get to work. It never happens that way. You get your butt in the chair (or wherever you're doing your work) and start letting

---

[35] If you don't know Malcolm Gladwell, he is one of the best-selling authors of the 21st century. Gladwell books we've covered on our podcast include: *Outliers, Talking To Strangers, The Tipping Point, What The Dog Saw, David and Goliath,* and *Blink.*

CONCLUSION | *Take Your Turn*

ideas rip. Good ideas, bad ideas, horrendously awful ideas... it's not your job to judge the ideas yet. Your only job right now is to produce *ideas*. You can weed out the duds later. After you produce, you can curate, you can select, and you can censor. But for now, be willing to have bad ideas. Lots and lots of bad ideas.

The rule is simple: the person who fails the most wins. If I fail more than you do, I will win. Because to keep failing, you've got to be good enough to keep playing. If you fail so badly that you never play again, you only fail once. But if you are always putting your work into the world, creating things, starting things, and taking your turn... your bad ideas will eventually become good ideas. You will learn along the way, learn to be more accurate, and learn the difference between what will work and what won't. But most importantly, you'll be out there, creating things in the real world, taking your turn.

How To Take Your Turn

1. Timing: It's Always Too Soon

When I (Jonesy) was a graduate starting my first job, we had a guest presenter come in during our first week to give us a little inspiration. I was sitting with a bunch of other fresh graduates. We'd gone to the best universities, got the best grades, had successful parents and had all the right connections in our network that had led us to be in this room. Dressed in our crisp new suits, it seemed the world held infinite options for our futures: family options, career options, geography options - the world was our oyster, and we could choose just about anything we wanted.

After listening to a half-hour presentation on metaphorical broken escalators and about how we could choose to do our very best work, the speaker urged us to become more than just a cog in a machine. Then one bloke named Tim raised his hand and said: *"But maybe it makes sense to wait? After all, we have student loans to pay off. It doesn't make sense to take risks now... later, when we're better established in our positions, and we're on a career track that is helping us climb up the ladder, THEN we can find our own path."*

But that's the thing... it's *never* the right time. When you're starting a new job, it's not the right time. When you're about to get a promotion, it's not the right time. When you're starting a family, it's not the right time. When your kids are about to go to college, it's not the right time. When you've got elderly parents who depend on you...

We have thousands of perfectly good reasons to play it safe and *not* take our turn. Of course it's safer and more comfortable to do it *later*. But this is the chance of a lifetime, *your* lifetime. Not someone else, you. Not later, now.

CONCLUSION | *Take Your Turn*

500 years ago, Gutenberg launched the printing press. What a foolish time to bring a book manufacturing system to the world... 96% of the population couldn't read!! When less than 1-in-25 people knew how to use the product, and when the skill to use it takes years to develop (learning how to read), it seems ridiculous that this project was even considered, let alone started! Surely books were never going to take off... What an idiot!

150 years ago, Karl Benz introduced the car to Germany. What a foolish time to launch a car... it was against the law to drive one!! He had to get a letter signed by the King granting him permission just to use this new machine. No one knew how to drive - most people had no idea what a car was. There were no roads and no gas stations. Another foolish project. Surely cars were never going to be popular... What an idiot!

There's a fundamental difference between being 'ready' and being 'prepared.' While you probably don't feel *ready* yet, you are more prepared than you realise. If you're trying to do something worthwhile, if you're trying to take your turn, to be bold enough to face your fears and try something new, you're never going to be ready.

Maybe your foolish idea isn't so foolish after all, and maybe you are more ready than you think.

2. Thirst

Where does thirst come from? It's almost impossible to go to a class and be taught to be thirsty for knowledge. It's almost impossible to read a book that ignites desire deep inside you. Thirst comes from habits: the habit of asking why, the habit of producing, the habit of launching, and the habit of leading. Everyone, regardless of background or culture, is capable of becoming thirsty. It's not based on gender or race or income, or even a desire to win. In fact, to take our turn, thirst is a requirement.

Where does the thirst go? Fear is the thirst killer. Extinguishing someone's thirst is quite easy. Simply punish them for asking why. Focus on grades and outcomes, not processes. Correct grammar instead of rewarding inquiry. Consume instead of produce. Give blame instead of taking responsibility.

What's better - finding out you got an 'A' or learning something new? It's quite a profound fork in the road. Our education system makes us shit-scared of looking down at a 'C.' The entire point of 13 or 17 years of our lives isn't to learn anything; it's to get an 'A.' Any wonder why our thirst disappears?

Instead, let's opt for a different path, the path of always learning and growing. In the armed forces, they have a process called 'hot wash' - at the end of every exercise, they get together to discuss what could go better next time. This room full of people working together to learn and improve is very different from a room full of people competing to get an 'A' on the test.

"I'm curious" is a completely different way of thinking than *"is everything going to be okay?"* Because everything is rarely okay... and that's okay.

3. Using Your Microphone

When they write the history of this current revolution we're living through, the one that started 20 years ago and continues to gain steam, they might mention the rise of online retail or the iPhone. But the most important thing that has happened is you've been given a microphone. We all have[36]. The most essential uses of the internet are all the same: email, chat, video, Meetup, TikTok, Instagram, eBay, Wikipedia, Kickstarter... every one of them gives you an opportunity to speak up and be heard. These new platforms are destroying the bottleneck of the requirement to be picked, to be given your turn by some powerful overlord, and are instead opening the door for you to pick yourself, to take your turn, to share, and to be generous.

Previously, if you wanted your voice to be heard, a newspaper or radio station or TV show had to pick you. Previously, if you made a product, a big retailer had to choose you to put it on their shelves. Now, we have the power to do

---

[36] For podcasters and YouTubers, it's a literal microphone. For everyone else, we're talking about metaphorical microphones.

CONCLUSION | *Take Your Turn*

these things without being picked by an organisation but by picking ourselves.

The invention of the microphone, the cheap, powerful, ubiquitous, metaphorical microphone that exists across every industry - changes everything.

When did you lose your voice? All these microphones, all this amplification... and we're stuck, unable to use them. Not because the microphone doesn't work but because we're unwilling to speak up. The internet has given anyone with something to say the freedom to say it. It has given us the freedom to connect, the freedom to produce, and the freedom to make a difference.

Yet we (all of us) refuse to use this freedom to its fullest. Because we can't bear to live with the internal narrative it would create, the narrative of responsibility and risk and failure. You haven't lost your voice. Your voice is there; it always has been. We're just paralysed. We can't make the fear or the feeling of dread go away; we can't fight it. Instead, we must acknowledge that it's always going to be there and then speak up regardless.

Is it easy? Of course not. If it were easy, you'd already be doing it. Just as the marathon runner is exhausted but keeps running anyway, the person with a loud and clear voice is afraid, but she speaks up regardless.

First, it can be a whisper, but you must be willing to say *something*.

It's Your Turn. So What Are You Going To Do?

It's not your turn to *win*. It's not your turn to be *picked*. It's not even your turn to get a guaranteed pat on the back if you have a crack.

It's merely your turn to try something. It's your turn to start walking up that escalator with your own two feet.

It's your turn to craft a vision, start making change, learn something new, conquer fear and be bold. It's your turn to shift your attitude.

if you liked this book, here's another for your reading list...

What You Can Learn From Books.

the sh*t they never taught you.

Adam Jones & Adam Ashton

Have you ever stumbled upon a piece of life-changing knowledge that made you think: why the hell didn't someone tell me this sooner?!

Millions of people have listened to Adam and Adam on the **What You Will Learn** podcast, where they have spent tens of thousands of hours studying the best ideas from the greatest minds on the planet. Their most frequently asked question: what is the best lesson you've come across? While you'd think a simple question would have a simple answer, it didn't - until now!

The Sh*t They Never Taught You will take you on a journey through takeaways from over a hundred of the world's greatest thinkers capturing lessons in personal development, career, business, personal finances, human nature, history, and philosophy. Every lesson will be useful, and one might change your life.

---

www.theshittheynevertaughtyou.com